新东方
XDF.CN

MW01687574

郭鹏 周亚 杜鹏 编著

SAT 巴朗词表学练测

浙江教育出版社·杭州

图书在版编目(CIP)数据

SAT巴朗词表学练测 / 郭鹏, 周亚, 杜鹃编著. -- 杭州 : 浙江教育出版社, 2017.12
ISBN 978-7-5536-6270-1

Ⅰ. ①S… Ⅱ. ①郭… ②周… ③杜… Ⅲ. ①英语－词汇－高等学校－入学考试－美国－习题集 Ⅳ. ①H313-44

中国版本图书馆CIP数据核字(2017)第216900号

SAT巴朗词表学练测
SAT BALANG CIBIAO XUE LIAN CE
郭鹏 周亚 杜鹃 编著

责任编辑 罗 曼
文字编辑 张 茜
美术编辑 韩 波
封面设计 尤媛媛
责任校对 刘文芳
责任印务 时小娟
版式设计 李 倩
出版发行 浙江教育出版社
地址：杭州市天目山路40号
邮编：310013
电话：（0571）85170300－80928
邮箱：dywh@xdf.cn
网址：www.zjeph.com
印 刷 三河市龙大印装有限公司
开 本 710mm×1000mm 1/16
成品尺寸 168mm×230mm
印 张 9.5
字 数 147 000
版 次 2017年12月第1版
印 次 2017年12月第1次印刷
标准书号 ISBN 978-7-5536-6270-1
定 价 30.00元

感谢以下老师对本书编写及出版的大力支持

刘烁炀　徐　静　田　甜

陈慧琳　贾思婕

序一
PREFACE

飞得更高

1872年的夏天，中国留学史正式拉开序幕。“中国留学之父”容闳组织了第一批幼童赴美留学。此后至1875年，清政府每年遴选30名少年渡洋深造，4年共派出120名。遥想当年，没人愿意出国留学，尚未开眼看世界的中国人，认为西方人是茹毛饮血的“蛮人”。接踵而来的战争惊醒沉醉于“天朝上国”迷梦的国人，留学热潮高涨。有19世纪末的留英法德热潮，有20世纪初的留日热潮，五四运动后的留法热潮，许多热血学子远渡重洋，吸取西方先进的社科文化。季羡林先生曾说过：“对中国近代化来说，留学生可以比作报春鸟，比作普罗米修斯，他们的功绩是永存的。”如今，随着国力的增强，中产阶级日益壮大，普通百姓有条件把孩子送出去，接受更加完整、有创造意义的高等教育。然而历经沧桑始终不变的是，这些留学生的发展牵系着祖国的腾飞。新东方在历史的浪潮里，承担着一种说不清道不明的使命，兢兢业业地助力一批又一批学子更高更远地飞翔。

教育部公布的数字显示，2016年中国有54万多学生出国深造，其中出国攻读本科学历的学生占到了3成多。中国的父母越来越具备国际眼光，愿意摆脱高考的独木桥，给孩子更多的选择、更广阔的发展空间。我很高兴看到我们有越来越多的优秀的同学走出国门，去到国外更广阔的世界。我一直鼓励学生们要多读书、多旅行、多交往、多思考，而出国留学正是很好的实现自我的方式。现在的孩子日益展现出他们独立思考和奋发追求自己人生目标的能力。我认为90后、00后及未来的10后，都凸显了我们这一代人没有的能力。他们更加有自己的判断力，有明确且卓越的志向。此外，他们大多很独立，愿意把所有的事情放到桌面上来谈，更加愿意主张自己的权利，更加愿意自觉地完善自己。就像无数位通过自身努力获得SAT、ACT考试高分的学生那样，他们都还那么年轻，却已经是国内最优秀的中学生。他们通过自己的努力考取了世界上最知名的高校，但学习优异并不是他们的全部，他们首先是立体的、丰富的人。他们的思想，他们对于世界的看法，对于理想的追求和执着，这一切不仅体现了新一代生生不息的生命力，而且为他们的同龄人提供了榜样的力量，这也让我们更加放心地让他们独自去更远、更加充满挑战的地方书写自己的精彩。

新东方倡导“终身学习，全球视野，独立人格”，真正的学习生涯，并不只是求知甚至是求成功的华山一条路，更应该求真求实，培养理性精神和健全人格。在越来越多的年轻人选择的留学之路上，新东方希望能提供最大的辅助，使更多的年轻人可以海阔天空施展自己的才华，可以热情专注研究自己的爱好，可以拓展自己的思维，可以好好阅读、争论、探究，让自己“独立之精神、自由之思想”开花结果。

俞敏洪

新东方教育科技集团董事长

序二

PREFACE

2016年初，SAT考试在新东方进入了一个“战略元年”，赶在老SAT退出之际，新东方教育科技集团统筹了全国性的教研规划，备战艰难的考试过渡期。在改革初期，SAT考试组织方美国大学理事会为减弱考试内容的培训机制，将老SAT考试中中国考生的“硬得分”部分（填空部分）完全去掉，以更为强调能力的“语境中理解单词”考法取而代之，使得大部分考生进入了一个周期漫长的适应过程。

为了更好地适应SAT考试的改革，引导学生从单纯地训练应试技巧逐步转化为关注实际能力的提升，新东方教育科技集团进行了教育产品上的一系列变革，其中一项重要任务就是建立完整的平台系统沉淀学生数据和学习轨迹以供教学产品设计参考。因此，管理、研究、使用学生数据在考试改革初期成为了推广中心的一项重要工作。具体地，词汇端的教学也积累了丰富的数据经验，从而进一步促成了这本学练测的编著。

以新东方第一批SAT学生为例，我们发现，他们中有很多在背完巴朗的经典词汇后依然难以应对改革后的SAT考试，传统的死记硬背词汇书的自学方式已经不适合现在的学生。巴朗的经典词汇难度较大，但是如何让这些词汇的学习适应改革后SAT考试的需求，这成为了我们应用数据、结合实际教研、跨科目设计产品的一项教学突破。这本学练测也就应运而生了。本书的选择题、搭配题、填空题由新东方骨干词汇老师和阅读老师共同完成，重在帮助考生梳理日常学习中所使用的单词，以便精准识记单词，进一步将所学词汇落实在语境中进行检验，尤其是SAT阅读考试需要掌握的词汇。由于巴朗词表的难度偏高，我们还设计了偏难词自测练习，帮助学生重复记忆，增强词汇学习效果，完成在美本考试中的词汇学习。

新东方存在的价值，是提供高效的教学服务，帮助考生提升学习效率，减少学习时间，有更多的时间去体验生活的美；对于美本申请的准留学生而言，则是有更多的时间去做提升自己申请背景厚度的事情。这本学练测的编写目的就在于，辅助《SAT巴朗词表：乱序版》，减少学生学习SAT的时间，至少可以提高背单词的效率。如果能够切实做到这一点，编者的良苦用心也就没有白费。愿广大考生能真正受益于本书的学习。

刘烁炀

新东方教育科技集团

国外考试推广管理中心主任

本书使用说明
How to Use This Book

众所周知，在美本学术类考试（SAT或ACT）中，词汇的学习一直是考生在提分上的一个痛点，究其原因主要有三点：第一，词汇难度远远超过中国高中水平；其二，即便通过反复的记忆，考生也难以学会如何正确使用，这就好比在中国高考语文科目中让考生去分辨“安排”和“安置”具体是怎么使用的；最后，不同语境中同一个单词会有不同的意思，例如我们的考生往往没有办法理解为什么“学校”（school）这个单词居然也能用来表示“派系”的意思。因此，为了让考生尽快地适应巴朗词汇的难度，完成更有效的单词学习，新东方教育科技集团国外考试推广管理中心核心教研人员研发出品了这本《SAT巴朗词表学练测》。本书为《SAT巴朗词表：乱序版》的配套练习，针对书中22个词表中的2136个核心词[1]、365个高频词、175个热词设计出符合考生学习轨迹和有效提高学习效率的单词练习，为SAT备考打下坚实的基础。

每个词表，按照由简到难设计了符合学生记忆规律的三个练习，建议考生（默认为第一次学习巴朗单词）采用以下学习方法：

① 时间安排：每个词表的单词数在100左右，可以分两种方法完成**词义记忆**，时间建议为：早上一半，下午一半，晚上测；或者分两天完成，第一天背，第二天测。由于巴朗词汇难度较高，对于初学者来说，建议按以上方法学习。

② 学完怎么测？

本书对每个词表设计了三个练习，考生需要按顺序完成这三个练习，以下为学习步骤：

a）在完成上面要求的**词义记忆**之后，考生应使用每个词表后面的Exercise A（练习1—选择题）来完成对词义记忆准确性的检测，我们对标了在考试中出现的高频单词，对于这一部分词来说，词义的记忆是最基本、最重要的。在完成练习A之后，考生当天的词汇任务结束，不再继续下一个练习[2]。

b）接下来，考生进入了第二天的单词学习，考生应该先复习前一天的**整个**词表，再进入新的词表学习，学习时间要保持一致，不要增加，不要减少。在复习和新词表学习任务结束之后，考生需要使用**前一个词表**的Exercise B （练习B—填空题

1）SAT考试改革后，巴朗词表从原来的3500个单词减少为2136个单词，由于改革后考纲有变，学生一定要使用新的巴朗词表。
——笔者注

2）我们设计这个练习是基于对词汇的难度、使用率和考生的记忆曲线、记忆的单词数量和测试强度的综合考虑，整体要适中才会提高单词的记忆效率，背得牢才会学得好。
——笔者注

或搭配题）和**新词表**的Exercise A（练习1—选择题）。每个词表中的练习B是针对SAT考试的"语境中理解词意"或"熟词僻义"这一要求来设计的。在填空题中，我们设计较简单的例句和语境，人工"降维"语境的难度，因为过于学术的句子并不适合巴朗单词的初学者和自学者。在此，考生进入了词汇的交叉学习，符合考生在词汇上的学习需求，背得更扎实。在搭配题中，我们设计选用了常考的熟词僻义来帮助考生再次巩固、加深对词义的理解和掌握。

c）第三天的学习，考生应该复习**前两天**的词表，再进入新的词表学习。学习时间要保持一致，不要增加，不要减少。在此，考生已经完成了**三个**词表的学习。在旧词表复习和新词表学习结束之后，考生需要使用**第一个词表**的Exercise C（练习3—偏难词自测练习）、第二个词表的Exercise B（练习2—填空题或搭配题）、第三个词表的Exercise A（练习1—选择题）。每完成任何一个Exercise C（练习3—偏难词自测练习），考生需要自己回到《SAT巴朗词表：乱序版》的词表**去对答案**[3]，并在本书练习前面的词表checklist中标注出自己没有写出的单词（用荧光笔标出或整理在笔记本上），循环复习，由于Exercise C中词汇较多，难度较大，考生可以分两次完成Exercise C。

d）因此，如果考生把一个词表拆成早晚两次背完，或者两天背完，那么3天或者6天将是完成一组记忆曲线强度的周期，这个周期可以根据考生自己的时间再拆（比如考生也可以拆成3次背完一个词表），但是一旦设定好初始的周期（背完一个词表的时间），就不要再随意增加或减少时间，要保证持续的强度和周期训练。

在此，作为新东方的集团培训师和美本高级教研员，我谨代表推广中心感谢在这过程中付出了艰辛劳动的郭鹏老师、周亚老师，以及全国各校的美本骨干教师在教学上兢兢业业的耕耘，没有他们的无私分享和多年的丰富教学经验作为基础，我们无法实现从产品内容的研究到以产品为导向的转变，设计出正确改进考生学习方法和行为的内容——这对于词汇的学习至关重要。

杜鹏

新东方教育科技集团国外考试推广管理中心

集团培训师、美本高级教研员

3）每个词表的练习A和B都设有答案，唯独C不设答案，目的是为了让考生能积累自己的学习数据，知道哪些词是自己不会的，标注好，循环复习。

——笔者注

目录
CONTENTS

Exercises

选择·填空·搭配

Review: Word List 1

- □ expurgate
- □ yen
- □ flinch
- □ invincible
- □ antiquated
- □ subdued
- □ deft
- □ divergent
- □ fitful
- □ hiatus
- □ stint
- □ infuriate
- □ molecule
- □ reverent
- □ conspicuous
- □ discomposure
- □ dissemble
- □ concession
- □ esoteric
- □ antidote
- □ unique
- □ receptive
- □ imperious
- □ intimidate
- □ retrograde
- □ meticulous
- □ toxic
- □ injurious
- □ acerbity
- □ condone
- □ rebuttal
- □ irreproachable
- □ economy
- □ agenda
- □ indelible
- □ insubordination
- □ repeal
- □ tangential
- □ halting
- □ nonchalance
- □ bode
- □ elusive
- □ correlation
- □ remunerative
- □ statute
- □ convention
- □ nullify
- □ remedial
- □ bemoan
- □ superficial
- □ rectify
- □ fabricate
- □ ordinance
- □ incorrigible
- □ stigmatize
- □ dwindle
- □ mediocre
- □ xenophobia
- □ wax
- □ emulate
- □ construe
- □ harbor
- □ disband
- □ consecrate
- □ entail
- □ relevant
- □ ulterior
- □ alias
- □ retrench
- □ grouse
- □ provincial
- □ wily
- □ contention
- □ incisive
- □ reprehensible
- □ mode
- □ desultory
- □ conglomeration
- □ enterprising
- □ animosity
- □ invulnerable
- □ fraternize
- □ dauntless
- □ metropolis
- □ dissent
- □ copious
- □ obsolete
- □ alleviate
- □ opportune
- □ caliber
- □ contest
- □ surveillance
- □ derogatory
- □ husband
- □ oligarchy
- □ decelerate
- □ integrity
- □ tumult
- □ fallacious

Exercise 1

Exercise 1-A Multiple-Choice Quiz (5 minutes)

Please choose the best answer that conveys the meaning of the given word. There is only one correct choice.
请根据所给单词的意思，从A,B,C,D四个选项中找出其同义词，每题只有一个正确答案。

1. esoteric (*adj*)
A. ecstatic
B. outside
C. obscure
D. eccentric

2. imperious (*adj*)
A. haughty
B. fallacious
C. unique
D. relevant

3. caliber (*n*)
A. cable
B. ability
C. expert
D. contest

4. integrity (*n*)
A. ingredient
B. tangent
C. intensity
D. honesty

5. consecrate (*v*)
A. rectify
B. sanctify
C. condone
D. consent

6. reverent (*adj*)
A. provincial
B. revengeful
C. respectful
D. receptive

7. intimidate (*v*)
A. intimate
B. fabricate
C. harbor
D. frighten

8. bemoan (*v*)
A. lament
B. mock
C. behold
D. anger

9. infuriate (*v*)
A. intrigue
B. ferry
C. enrage
D. infuse

10. dissemble (*v*)
A. dismiss
B. disguise
C. dislike
D. dissent

11. stigmatize (*v*)
A. brand
B. stimulate
C. simulate
D. stagnate

12. deft (*adj*)
A. adept
B. neat
C. dexterous
D. all of the above

13. dwindle (*v*)
A. discard
B. shrink
C. discompose
D. entail

14. animosity (*n*)
A. enmity
B. contention
C. rebuttal
D. agenda

15. construe (*v*)
A. content
B. consent
C. conserve
D. explain

16. ordinance (*n*)
A. sequence
B. statute
C. commonness
D. request

17. reprehensible (*adj*)
A. understandable
B. representative
C. deplorable
D. obsolete

Exercise 1-B Sentence-Completion Quiz (30 minutes)

Please fill in the blanks, choosing the words from the list. Each word can only be used once.
请从表格所列单词中选出最符合语境的单词，填入空格，每个单词只能使用一次。

Word List

antiquated	*indelible*	*insubordination*	*surveillance*	*discomposure*
contest	*meticulous*	*tangential*	*alleviate*	
ulterior	*stint*	*halting*	*fraternize*	
superficial	*injurious*	*emulate*	*invulnerable*	
nonchalance	*elusive*	*wily*	*opportune*	

1. International Criminal Police Organization have searched all the corners of the earth for the ______ hijackers.
2. Some journalists criticize her ______ and indifference.
3. Foxes are supposed to be ______ creatures.
4. He couldn't prevent her pain, only ______ it.
5. His varied career included a ______ as a magician.
6. I believe that I have arrived at a very ______ moment.
7. You must work hard to ______ your brother's success.
8. My visit to India in 1986 left an ______ impression on me.
9. He pleaded no ______ to two misdemeanor counts.
10. Smoking is ______ to health, especially to the lungs.
11. Many factories are so ______ that they are not worth saving.
12. I am sure under your ______ care these trees will flourish day by day.
13. Everyone's emotion contains ______ and anxiety.
14. No state in the region is ______ to attack by another.
15. Too much time was spent discussing ______ issues.
16. He found himself put under ______ by the country's military intelligence.
17. In Los Angeles in 1973, one secretary was fired for "incompetence, ______ and failure to comply with job instructions" after refusing to make coffee.
18. Staff were warned not to ______ with reporters from other newspapers.
19. I suspect he may have had ______ motives for being so generous.
20. Shyness made the girl speak in a ______ manner.
21. I know well how slight is my talent and how ______ my scholarship, and that I do not deserve so much praise.

Exercise 1-C 偏难词自测练习 (30 minutes)

Please fill in the blanks, choosing the words from the list. Each word can only be used once. Then you can go back to the Word List and check your answers.
请从表格所列单词中选出与下列中文意思对应的单词，填入空格，每个单词只能使用一次。完毕之后，请回到《SAT巴朗词表：乱序版》中对应的单元，核对答案，并标注自己没有填对的单词。

Word List

expurgate	receptive	statute	relevant	dissent
yen	retrograde	convention	alias	copious
flinch	toxic	nullify	retrench	obsolete
invincible	acerbity	remedial	grouse	derogatory
subdued	condone	rectify	provincial	husband
divergent	rebuttal	fabricate	contention	oligarchy
fitful	irreproachable	incorrigible	incisive	decelerate
hiatus	economy	mediocre	mode	tumult
molecule	agenda	xenophobia	desultory	fallacious
conspicuous	repeal	wax	conglomeration	
concession	bode	harbor	enterprising	
antidote	correlation	disband	dauntless	
unique	remunerative	entail	metropolis	

寡头政治 oligarchy

吵闹，骚动 tumult

谬误的；误导的 fallacious

减速 decelerate

侮辱的，贬义的 derogatory

中等的，平庸的 mediocre

习俗，惯例 convention

纠正，改正 rectify

变大，增大 wax

解散，遣散 disband

时尚，风尚；方式，方法；风格 mode

锋利的，尖锐的 incisive

埋怨，发牢骚 grouse

不同意，持异议 dissent

瘾；渴望 yen

畏缩，退缩 flinch

缓和的；柔和的 subdued

废除，撤销 repeal

倒退，退化 retrograde

有报酬的，有利的 remunerative

大胆的；不屈不挠的 dauntless

无可救药的，不能被纠正的 incorrigible

制造；编造 fabricate

使无效，废除 nullify

法令，条例 statute

仇外者，惧外者 xenophobia

要求，使必要；牵涉 entail

主张，论点 contention

团块，混合物 conglomeration

省的，偏狭的；守旧的 provincial

有事业的，有进取精神的 enterprising

紧缩；节约 retrench
不再使用的，过时的 antiquated obsolete
删改，删节 expurgate
间歇的，断断续续的 fitful
议事日程 agenda
辩驳，举反证 rebuttal
预示 bode
分子；小颗粒 molecule
有毒的，中毒的 toxic
宽恕，赦免 condone
散漫的，随便的，离题的 desultory
别名，化名 alias
相应的，相关联的 relevant
治疗的；补救的 remedial
大城市，都会 metropolis

丰富的 copious
不可战胜的 invincible
有分歧的；分叉的 divergent
让步，妥协 concession
解毒剂 antidote
无可指责的，无瑕疵的 irreproachable
唯一的，独特的 unique
节约，节俭 economy
善于接受的，能接纳的 receptive
裂缝；间断 hiatus
明显的，显著的 conspicuous
相关，相互关系 correlation
尖酸，刻薄 acerbity
提供住所或栖息地；窝藏 harbor
节约使用 husband

Review: Word List 2

- □ inhibit
- □ reciprocal
- □ adapt
- □ ordeal
- □ analogy
- □ ferment
- □ materialism
- □ suffragist
- □ embellish
- □ recalcitrant
- □ penury
- □ mischance
- □ oblivious
- □ clientele
- □ repel
- □ sovereign
- □ shoddy
- □ recant
- □ shirk
- □ impeach
- □ aversion
- □ abate
- □ destitute
- □ magnitude
- □ predetermine
- □ incorporate
- □ subjugate
- □ adverse
- □ heckler
- □ increment
- □ ebullient
- □ calculated
- □ indoctrinate
- □ stealth
- □ generate
- □ preeminent
- □ stifle
- □ connotation
- □ berserk
- □ matrix
- □ paraphrase
- □ redress
- □ spatial
- □ lament
- □ extant
- □ perpetual
- □ conspiracy
- □ annul
- □ utopia
- □ flourish
- □ compliance
- □ inert
- □ forebear
- □ restitution
- □ frantic
- □ aggrandize
- □ forthright
- □ prelude
- □ immutable
- □ upshot
- □ multifaceted
- □ pariah
- □ tantamount
- □ labyrinth
- □ appease
- □ doctrinaire
- □ belligerent
- □ somber
- □ divulge
- □ bungle
- □ premise
- □ render
- □ automaton
- □ illuminate
- □ disabuse
- □ craftiness
- □ assent
- □ exotic
- □ extrapolation
- □ salutary
- □ anomaly
- □ delusion
- □ mock
- □ reconnaissance
- □ transitory
- □ accessory
- □ lucid
- □ delude
- □ dismantle
- □ depravity
- □ manipulate
- □ tangible
- □ rapport
- □ influx
- □ eclipse
- □ gist
- □ unequivocal
- □ mandatory
- □ persevere
- □ stalemate

Exercise 2

Exercise 2-A **Multiple-Choice Quiz (5 minutes)**

Please choose the best answer that conveys the meaning of the given word. There is only one correct choice.
请根据所给单词的意思，从A,B,C,D四个选项中找出其同义词，每题只有一个正确答案。

1. adverse (*adj*)
A. versatile
B. hostile
C. abrupt
D. advantageous

2. appease (*v*)
A. pacify
B. appall
C. apply
D. trace

3. stealth (*n*)
A. steel
B. secretiveness
C. theft
D. stead

4. divulge (*v*)
A. reveal
B. divide
C. divert
D. diverge

5. belligerent (*adj*)
A. legal
B. fanciful
C. quarrelsome
D. tremendous

6. delude (*v*)
A. allude
B. elude
C. shirk
D. deceive

7. oblivious (*adj*)
A. calculated
B. imperious
C. obvious
D. unmindful

8. perpetual (*adj*)
A. everlasting
B. transient
C. appropriate
D. competent

9. forthright (*adj*)
A. forward
B. frank
C. correct
D. inert

10. somber (*adj*)
A. unruffled
B. sober
C. gloomy
D. frantic

11. aggrandize (*v*)
A. aggregate
B. intensify
C. grant
D. generate

12. stifle (*v*)
A. steal
B. inhibit
C. strip
D. serve

13. impeach (*v*)
A. impart
B. impress
C. indict
D. innovate

14. subjugate (*v*)
A. submit
B. convene
C. conquer
D. substitute

15. immutable (*adj*)
A. communicative
B. mandatory
C. multifaceted
D. unchangeable

16. persevere (*v*)
A. persist
B. profess
C. prosper
D. perceive

17. eclipse (*v*)
A. collapse
B. surpass
C. execute
D. escalate

18. illuminate (*v*)
A. embody
B. collaborate
C. enlighten
D. connect

19. salutary (*adj*)
A. salty
B. saline
C. tangible
D. wholesome

Exercise 2-B　Matching Quiz (5 minutes)

Match the words from the two columns.
从右边列表中选出和左边单词意思匹配的词汇，把它们用线连起来。

Ⓐ

embellish	similarity
analogy	meaning
ferment	conformity
compliance	unite
connotation	turmoil
incorporate	ornament

Ⓑ

ebullient	outstanding
reciprocal	decrease
aversion	introduction
conspiracy	joyful
preeminent	disgust
abate	mutual
sovereign	increase
increment	dislike
prelude	plot
repel	self-governing

Ⓒ

assent	postulate
anomaly	intelligible
depravity	deliver
lucid	irregularity
extrapolation	projection
premise	accept
render	corruption

Exercise 2-C　偏难词自测练习 (30 minutes)

Please fill in the blanks, choosing the words from the list. Each word can only be used once. Then you can go back to the Word List and check your answers.
请从表格所列单词中选出与下列中文意思对应的单词，填入空格，每个单词只能使用一次。完毕之后，请回到《SAT巴朗词表：乱序版》中对应的单元，核对答案，并标注自己没有填对的单词。

Word List

inhibit	destitute	lament	tantamount	accessory
adapt	magnitude	extant	labyrinth	dismantle
ordeal	predetermine	annul	doctrinaire	manipulate
materialism	heckler	utopia	bungle	tangible
suffragist	calculated	flourish	automaton	rapport
recalcitrant	indoctrinate	inert	disabuse	influx
penury	generate	forebear	craftiness	gist
mischance	berserk	restitution	exotic	unequivocal
clientele	matrix	frantic	delusion	mandatory
shoddy	paraphrase	upshot	mock	stalemate
recant	redress	multifaceted	reconnaissance	
shirk	spatial	pariah	transitory	

乌托邦，理想的完美境界 utopia

狂暴的 berserk

抑制，限制，阻止 inhibit

贫穷，贫困 penury

苦难经历，折磨 ordeal

妇女政权论者 suffragist

以教条或信条的方式来教授，教导 indoctrinate

废除，取消 annul

熟练地操作；巧妙地处理 manipulate

明确的，不含糊的 unequivocal

去除…的谬误，使醒悟 disabuse

搞糟；笨手笨脚地做 bungle

狡猾 craftiness

流入 influx

尚存的，现存的 extant

激烈质问者 heckler

意译，改述 paraphrase

狂乱的，疯狂的 frantic

撤回，放弃；撤回声明；公开认错 recant

嘲弄，以模仿的方式嘲笑 muck

产生；发生 generate

补救，补偿 redress

[illegible]利主义，物质主义 materialism

与…相当的 tantamount

机器人；机械般行动的人或动物 automation

为…悲痛，痛惜 lament

巨大，重大 magnitude

彼此有爱的关系，和谐 rapport

要点，主旨 gist

贫困的，赤贫的 destitute

结果，结局 upshot

多层面的 multifaceted

劣质的；廉价的 shoddy

预先决定，预先倾向 predetermine

惰性的；迟钝的，迟缓的 inert

社会的遗弃者 pariah

顾客，常客 clientele

转瞬即逝的，短暂的 transitory

归还；赔偿；修复 recant restitution

使适应，顺应；改写 adapt

顽抗的，桀骜不驯的 recalcitrant

逃避，推卸 Shirk

空间的 spatial

不幸，灾难 mischance

迷宫 labyrinth

拆开，解散 dismantle

命令的，强制的 mandatory

可触知的；真实的 tangible

繁荣；茂盛；装饰 flourish

附件，附属物，配饰 accessory

母体，发源地；矩阵；模型，模具 matrix

异国情调的；奇异的 exotic

有计划的；可能的 Calculated

教条主义的；不屈的，不让步的 doctrinaire

错觉，幻觉 delusion

侦查，勘察 reconnaissance

祖先，祖宗 forebear

僵局 stalemate

Review: Word List 3

- □ nefarious
- □ stratagem
- □ aggregate
- □ apposite
- □ validate
- □ credo
- □ disingenuous
- □ slander
- □ liability
- □ accessible
- □ deviate
- □ prolong
- □ centrifugal
- □ erode
- □ dishearten
- □ mnemonic
- □ convert
- □ acrid
- □ retroactive
- □ congruent
- □ emendation
- □ duplicity
- □ foster
- □ arcane
- □ defunct
- □ tactile
- □ anesthetic
- □ multilingual
- □ artless
- □ etymology
- □ verbose
- □ vilify
- □ apprehension
- □ dictum
- □ quench
- □ expedient
- □ corrode
- □ rejuvenate
- □ pivotal
- □ notoriety
- □ prototype
- □ practicable
- □ impending
- □ unimpeachable
- □ codify
- □ discount
- □ brandish
- □ animated
- □ deplete
- □ felicity
- □ circumscribe
- □ rant
- □ foolhardy
- □ decoy
- □ domineer
- □ adulterate
- □ awe
- □ ascetic
- □ retract
- □ adroit
- □ stolid
- □ succumb
- □ forum
- □ petty
- □ uniformity
- □ cater to
- □ prestige
- □ haphazard
- □ synoptic
- □ seismic
- □ extol
- □ embrace
- □ amnesia
- □ comeuppance
- □ lethal
- □ vindicate
- □ indifferent
- □ anticlimax
- □ material
- □ modicum
- □ maverick
- □ spendthrift
- □ incriminate
- □ feign
- □ brawn
- □ bane
- □ thwart
- □ archaeology
- □ addle
- □ pious
- □ optimist
- □ impeccable
- □ alacrity
- □ simplistic
- □ ancestry
- □ reputed
- □ fervor
- □ accommodate
- □ astute
- □ pantomime

Exercise 3

Exercise 3-A Multiple-Choice Quiz (5 minutes)

Please choose the best answer that conveys the meaning of the given word. There is only one correct choice.
请根据所给单词的意思，从A,B,C,D四个选项中找出其同义词，每题只有一个正确答案。

1. apposite (*adj*)
A. accessible
B. appreciable
C. appropriate
D. artless

2. disingenuous (*adj*)
A. insincere
B. distinguished
C. animated
D. practicable

3. prestige (*n*)
A. property
B. prediction
C. radiation
D. reputation

4. slander (*n*)
A. defamation
B. uniformity
C. sanity
D. strife

5. pivotal (*adj*)
A. pious
B. crucial
C. damp
D. crude

6. deviate (*v*)
A. prolong
B. erode
C. dishearten
D. diverge

7. circumscribe (*v*)
A. codify
B. limit
C. deplete
D. comply

8. impending (*adj*)
A. material
B. intrepid
C. approaching
D. linking

9. succumb (*v*)
A. embrace
B. accommodate
C. yield
D. cumber

10. vindicate (*v*)
A. elevate
B. illuminate
C. justify
D. deteriorate

11. validate (*v*)
A. critique
B. vanish
C. convert
D. confirm

12. feign (*v*)
A. forge
B. forgo
C. prepare
D. pretend

13. lethal (*adj*)
A. tidal
B. deadly
C. linguistic
D. sore

14. ascetic (*adj*)
A. aesthetic
B. seismic
C. austere
D. indifferent

15. extol (*v*)
A. glorify
B. extend
C. tolerate
D. command

16. petty (*adj*)
A. pretty
B. pure
C. trivial
D. stingy

Exercise 3-B Sentence-Completion Quiz (30 minutes)

Please fill in the blanks, choosing the words from the list. Each word can only be used once.
请从表格所列单词中选出最符合语境的单词，填入空格，每个单词只能使用一次。

Word List

retract	*liability*	*forum*	*felicity*	*domineer*
incriminate	*cater to*	*astute*	*thwart*	
congruent	*ancestry*	*awe*	*expedient*	
notoriety	*adulterate*	*brandish*	*reputed*	
stratagem	*discount*	*dictum*	*apprehension*	

1. Then they do something asinine, get in trouble and begin the downward slope out of fame into ______.
2. We shouldn't ______ the effect of AIDS.
3. They want to work in an organization whose values are ______ with their own.

4. As the president's prestige continues to fall, they're clearly beginning to consider him a liability.
5. Exercise classes cater to all levels of fitness.
6. He appeared in the lounge brandishing a knife.
7. Trade discounts may be used as a competitive stratagem to secure customer loyalty.
8. Her father promised her to spend the weekend with her at the seaside, but he retract the next day.
9. In his confession the thief incriminate two others who helped him steal.
10. The house is reputed to be the original of Mansfield Park.
11. It reflects real anger and apprehension about the future.
12. Big boys sometimes domineer over the younger pupils.
13. Our plans for a picnic were thwart by the rain.
14. The government found it expedient to relax censorship a little.
15. The letters page of this newspaper is a forum for public argument.
16. A dictum is a formal statement made by someone who has authority.
17. Most unwilling was she to awaken from such a dream of felicity to comprehend all the unhappy truths which attended the affair.
18. The family has traced its ancestry to the Norman invaders.
19. The food had been adulterate to increase its weight.
20. A good leader must be an astute judge of ability. One glance at a pyramid can leave the viewer in awe of its beauty and splendor.
21. One glance at a pyramid can leave the viewer in awe of its beauty and splendor.

Exercise 3-C 偏难词自测练习 (30 minutes)

Please fill in the blanks, choosing the words from the list. Each word can only be used once. Then you can go back to the Word List and check your answers.

请从表格所列单词中选出与下列中文意思对应的单词，填入空格，每个单词只能使用一次。完毕之后，请回到《SAT巴朗词表：乱序版》中对应的单元，核对答案，并标注自己没有填对的单词。

Word List

nefarious	duplicity	rejuvenate	haphazard	bane
aggregate	foster	prototype	synoptic	archaeology
credo	arcane	practicable	seismic	addle
accessible	defunct	unimpeachable	embrace	pious
prolong	tactile	codify	amnesia	optimist
centrifugal	anesthetic	animated	comeuppance	impeccable
erode	multilingual	deplete	indifferent	alacrity
dishearten	artless	rant	anticlimax	simplistic
mnemonic	etymology	foolhardy	material	fervor
convert	verbose	decoy	modicum	accommodate
acrid	vilify	adroit	maverick	pantomime
retroactive	quench	stolid	spendthrift	
emendation	corrode	uniformity	brawn	

记忆的，记忆性的 mnemonic

离心的 centrifugal

啰嗦的，唠叨的 verbose

抚育；鼓励 foster

侵蚀 corrode

编成法典，编纂；整理 codify

邪恶的，穷凶极恶的 nefarious

已死的，已灭绝的；失效的 defunct

能实行的，行得通的 practicable

熟练的，机敏的 adroit

过分单纯化的 simplistic

热情，热烈 fervor

咆哮，大声责骂；激昂地说，夸夸其谈 rant

同样，一致 uniformity

修改，改善 emendation

地震的 seismic

少量，一点点 modicum

熄灭，抑制（欲望）；满足 quench

报应 comeuppance

冷漠的，不关心的；一般的，中等的 indifferent

持不同意见者，独来独往者 maverick

易接近的，易得到的 accessible

使返老还童，使恢复活力 rejuvenate

使沮丧，使失去勇气或希望 dishearten

皈依者；皈依；使改变 convert

原型，样板 prototype

用完，耗尽 deplete

触觉的，有触觉的 tactile

信条 credo

无可指摘的，可做模范的 unimpeachable

虔诚的；宗教的 pious

不易激动的，感觉迟钝的 stolid
哑剧 pantomime
使用多种语言的 multilingual
祸根，灾星 bane
诽谤，诋毁 vilify
口是心非，搞两面派，欺骗；虚伪 duplicity
考古学 archaeology
物质的；具体的；重要的 material
偶然的，随意的；杂乱无章的 haphazard
肌肉的力量；强壮 brawn
无虚饰的；朴实的 artless
延长，拖延 prolong
神秘的；晦涩难懂的 arcane
尖刻的，辛辣的 acrid
侵蚀，腐蚀，削弱 erode
引诱；诱饵 decoy
使糊涂；腐坏 addle
无瑕疵的 impeccable
帮主，调节；使适应 accomodate
活生生的，活泼的 animated
乐观主义者 optimist
使聚集，积聚 aggregate
词源学 etymology
麻醉剂，麻药 anesthetic
愚勇的，莽撞的 foolhardy
敏捷，轻快；爽快，乐意 alacrity
记忆缺失，健忘症 amnesia
有追溯效力的 retroactic
提要的，摘要的 synoptic
拥抱；欣然采纳；包括 embrace
突降，虎头蛇尾 anticlimax
挥霍者 spendthrift

Review: Word List 4

- □ permeate
- □ exemplify
- □ worldly
- □ integrate
- □ pitfall
- □ expropriate
- □ table
- □ acquittal
- □ waive
- □ aspire
- □ legend
- □ abscond
- □ modulate
- □ doctrine
- □ conjecture
- □ negate
- □ redundant
- □ amenable
- □ informal
- □ candor
- □ marked
- □ impregnable
- □ detraction
- □ impiety
- □ muse
- □ impotent
- □ bland
- □ covenant
- □ indomitable
- □ mandate
- □ compatible
- □ geniality
- □ checkered
- □ dilute
- □ solicit
- □ indices
- □ iconoclastic
- □ pathetic
- □ immune
- □ intractable
- □ equanimity
- □ concede
- □ schematic
- □ caustic
- □ inordinate
- □ countermand
- □ eccentricity
- □ hoard
- □ sentinel
- □ chide
- □ comprise
- □ preempt
- □ exonerate
- □ flamboyant
- □ incipient
- □ differentiate
- □ parallelism
- □ abhor
- □ ambience
- □ servitude
- □ stanza
- □ amalgamate
- □ refute
- □ renege
- □ admonition
- □ interim
- □ effete
- □ incite
- □ acme
- □ compound
- □ insipid
- □ irrational
- □ burnish
- □ rampant
- □ repercussion
- □ underlying
- □ tycoon
- □ appreciate
- □ depredation
- □ preclude
- □ rabid
- □ parameter
- □ abyss
- □ incessant
- □ conscientious
- □ assiduous
- □ formality
- □ conviction
- □ fop
- □ chary
- □ venturesome
- □ query
- □ titanic
- □ wispy
- □ valor
- □ inevitable
- □ reactionary
- □ mitigate
- □ palpable
- □ assuage

Exercise 4

Exercise 4-A Multiple-Choice Quiz (5 minutes)

Please choose the best answer that conveys the meaning of the given word. There is only one correct choice.
请根据所给单词的意思，从A,B,C,D四个选项中找出其同义词，每题只有一个正确答案。

1. doctrine (*n*)
A. legend
B. dogma
C. parallelism
D. servitude

2. compatible (*adj*)
A. harmonious
B. marked
C. informal
D. irrational

3. negate (*n*)
A. nullify
B. muse
C. appreciate
D. neglect

4. hoard (*v*)
A. herd
B. roar
C. concede
D. store

5. caustic (*adj*)
A. worldly
B. corrosive
C. casual
D. undistinguished

6. exonerate (*v*)
A. exemplify
B. mandate
C. vindicate
D. differentiate

7. inordinate (*adj*)
A. excessive
B. immune
C. titanic
D. protracted

8. inevitable (*adj*)
A. exceptional
B. unequivocal
C. unavoidable
D. underlying

9. insipid (*adj*)
A. dauntless
B. dull
C. tactile
D. acrid

10. palpable (*adj*)
A. tangible
B. reliable
C. affordable
D. feasible

11. assiduous (*adj*)

A. synoptic
B. homogeneous
C. polished
D. diligent

12. preclude (*v*)

A. prevent
B. dilute
C. compound
D. precede

13. abhor (*v*)

A. aspire
B. detest
C. retract
D. manipulate

14. amalgamate (*v*)

A. amend
B. adopt
C. combine
D. compete

15. chide (*v*)

A. cheat
B. cherish
C. conceive
D. scold

16. impotent (*adj*)

A. weak
B. venturesome
C. efficient
D. deficient

17. waive (*v*)

A. modulate
B. abandon
C. necessitate
D. wind

18. conjecture (*v*)

A. contest
B. collide
C. surmise
D. surmount

19. solicit (*v*)

A. seek
B. pervade
C. exclaim
D. stipulate

20. flamboyant (*adj*)

A. flammable
B. abundant
C. tricky
D. showy

Exercise 4-B　Matching Quiz (5 minutes)

Match the words from the two columns.
从右边列表中选出和左边单词意思匹配的词汇，把它们用线连起来。

A

query	polish
burnish	include
admonition	question
pathetic	pitiful
comprise	warning

B

redundant	slander
countermand	atmosphere
parameter	superfluous
ambience	deferential
mitigate	boundary
detraction	cancel
amenable	appease
candor	friendliness
geniality	honesty

Exercise 4-C　偏难词自测练习 (30 minutes)

Please fill in the blanks, choosing the words from the list. Each word can only be used once. Then you can go back to the Word List and check your answers.
请从表格所列单词中选出与下列中文意思对应的单词，填入空格，每个单词只能使用一次。完毕之后，请回到《SAT巴朗词表：乱序版》中对应的单元，核对答案，并标注自己没有填对的单词。

Word List

permeate	table	informal	covenant	iconoclastic
exemplify	acquittal	marked	indomitable	immune
worldly	aspire	impregnable	mandate	intractable
integrate	legend	impiety	checkered	equanimity
pitfall	abscond	muse	dilute	concede
expropriate	modulate	bland	indices	schematic

eccentricity	refute	rampant	incessant	wispy
sentinel	renege	repercussion	conscientious	valor
preempt	interim	underlying	formality	reactionary
incipient	effete	tycoon	conviction	assuage
differentiate	incite	appreciate	fop	
parallelism	acme	depredation	chary	
servitude	compound	rabid	venturesome	
stanza	irrational	abyss	titanic	

地图的图例，插图的说明 legend

使音调转低；调节，调整；变调，转调 modulate

不尊敬，不虔诚 impiety

和蔼的；平和的 bland

平和，镇静 equanimity

免疫的；豁免的，免除的 immune

不屈服的，不屈不挠的 indomitable

承认，让出 concede

多变的，盛衰无常的 checkered

（企业界的）大亨，巨头 tycoon

中间时期，过渡时期 interim

使成整体，使一体化 integrate

指数，指标 indices

驳斥，驳倒 refute

抢劫，掠夺性攻击 depredation

搁置 table

感激；增值；体谅 appreciate

谨慎的；吝啬的 chary

有记号的；显眼的；成为攻击对象的 marked

区别，鉴别 differentiate

奴役；劳役 servitude

先占，先取；取代 preempt

渗透，弥漫 permeate

潜逃 abscond

图表的，图解的 schematic

隐患；陷阱 pitfall

契约 covenant

蔓延的；不受限制的 rampant

不断的，不停的 incessant

不合理的；无理性的；荒谬的 irrational

作为…的范例 examplify

深渊 abyss

缺乏活力的；软弱的，衰弱的；贫瘠的 effete

偶像破坏的，打破旧习的 iconoclastic

混合，组合；以复利计算；使增加 compound

稀释，冲淡；削弱 dilute

征用，没收 expropriate

仪式；礼节，俗套 formality

平行，类似 parallelism

不正式的，不拘礼节的 informal

花花公子；过分讲究衣饰或举动的人 fop

起初的，开始存在或出现的 incipient

冒险的，大胆的 venturesome

宣告有罪；深信 conviction

宣判无罪 acquittal

沉思，冥想；默想 muse

有志于，渴望 aspire

潜在的；根本的；在下面的 underlying

难以驾驭的，倔强的 intractable

疯狂的，狂热的 rabid

刺激，激励；煽动 incite

命令，训令；要求 mandate

影响；弹回；反响，回声 repercussion

尽责的，谨慎的 conscientious

世间的，尘世的 worldly

顶峰 acme

岗哨，看守；哨兵 sentinel

否认；违背，背弃 renege

巨大的 titanic

英勇，勇猛 valor

无懈可击的，固若金汤的 impregnable

反作用的；反动的，保守的 reactionary

减轻，使满足 assuage

古怪行为，反常行为 eccentricity

纤细的，脆弱的；细微的 wispy

（诗的）节 stanza

Review: Word List 5

- □ untenable
- □ vulnerable
- □ sever
- □ recourse
- □ fatalism
- □ realm
- □ relinquish
- □ surmount
- □ barricade
- □ chasten
- □ quorum
- □ entitlement
- □ impenetrable
- □ mores
- □ quintessence
- □ disaffected
- □ diversity
- □ sublime
- □ opus
- □ catalyst
- □ unwarranted
- □ furtive
- □ anthropologist
- □ sectarian
- □ leniency
- □ fathom
- □ denotation
- □ faze
- □ outmoded
- □ phlegmatic
- □ depose
- □ anonymous
- □ antithesis
- □ convene
- □ bolster
- □ intrinsic
- □ stupefy
- □ amnesty
- □ moribund
- □ incredulous
- □ impecunious
- □ cardinal
- □ rescind
- □ aboriginal
- □ expatriate
- □ ambiguous
- □ appall
- □ myriad
- □ benevolent
- □ exposure
- □ imply
- □ physiological
- □ relent
- □ renown
- □ disputatious
- □ aloof
- □ ideology
- □ circumlocution
- □ creed
- □ title
- □ premeditate
- □ recurrent
- □ fancy
- □ mediate
- □ blunder
- □ despot
- □ pandemonium
- □ prowess
- □ minute
- □ metamorphosis
- □ fledgling
- □ expertise
- □ ecologist
- □ rebuff
- □ malleable
- □ laud
- □ homogeneous
- □ fundamental
- □ ratiocination
- □ annex
- □ brunt
- □ chaotic
- □ cogent
- □ terminology
- □ ambulatory
- □ preamble
- □ kindle
- □ replete
- □ puerile
- □ fictitious

Exercise 5

Exercise 5-A　Multiple-Choice Quiz (5 minutes)

Please choose the best answer that conveys the meaning of the given word. There is only one correct choice.
请根据所给单词的意思，从A,B,C,D四个选项中找出其同义词，每题只有一个正确答案。

1. vulnerable (*adj*)
A. fertile
B. everlasting
C. punctual
D. attackable

2. disaffected (*adj*)
A. ineffective
B. disloyal
C. demanding
D. novel

3. leniency (*n*)
A. mildness
B. barricade
C. entitlement
D. recollection

4. quintessence (*n*)
A. epitome
B. deference
C. acquaintance
D. accommodation

5. sever (*v*)
A. stain
B. scatter
C. shatter
D. separate

6. untenable (*adj*)
A. myriad
B. disputatious
C. fundamental
D. indefensible

7. fathom (*v*)
A. comprehend
B. slit
C. scrutinize
D. enhance

8. depose (*v*)
A. supervise
B. resent
C. dethrone
D. deposit

9. furtive (*adj*)
A. fertile
B. ethnic
C. stealthy
D. routine

10. bolster (*v*)
A. interpret
B. distort
C. support
D. theorize

11. appall (*v*)
A. shock
B. intervene
C. vent
D. gratify

12. convene (*v*)
A. outwit
B. assemble
C. impulse
D. conflict

13. expatriate (*n*)
A. native
B. invader
C. walker
D. exile

14. phlegmatic (*adj*)
A. aesthetic
B. calm
C. taut
D. arbitrary

15. aboriginal (*adj*)
A. incidental
B. native
C. rigid
D. instinctive

16. intrinsic (*adj*)
A. impenetrable
B. homogeneous
C. physiological
D. inherent

17. replete (*adj*)
A. delusional
B. immune
C. colossal
D. full

18. fictitious (*adj*)
A. meticulous
B. immature
C. imaginary
D. chaotic

19. laud (*v*)
A. distend
B. praise
C. envy
D. elect

20. preamble (*n*)
A. civilization
B. aristocrat
C. introduction
D. presidency

21. cogent (*adj*)
A. minute
B. recurrent
C. benevolent
D. convincing

Exercise 5-B Sentence-Completion Quiz (30 minutes)

Please fill in the blanks, choosing the words from the list. Each word can only be used once.
请从表格所列单词中选出最符合语境的单词，填入空格，每个单词只能使用一次。

Word List

ambiguous	*recourse*	*incredulous*	*outmoded*	*anonymous*
aloof	*premeditate*	*realm*	*relinquish*	*impenetrable*
surmount	*malleable*	*circumlocution*	*cardinal*	
unwarranted	*mediate*	*sublime*	*kindle*	
denotation	*blunder*	*relent*	*prowess*	

1. Despite heavy winds and nearly ________ ground fog, the plane landed safely.
2. The king banished the traitor from the ________.
3. Something that is ________ does not reveal who you are.
4. A good dictionary will give us the connotation of a word as well as its ________.
5. I couldn't tell which direction without ________ to a map.
6. I realized I had to ________ the language barrier.
7. Random drug testing of employees is an ________ invasion of privacy.
8. He was forced to ________ control of the company and left.
9. As a salesman, your ________ rule is to do everything you can to satisfy a customer.
10. His works range from the ________ ridiculous, with very little in between.
11. "You told Pete?" Rachel said in an ________ voice, "I can't believe it!"
12. Technologies change rapidly and today's cutting edge may be tomorrow's ________ design.
13. If you describe something as ________, you mean that it is unclear or confusing because it can be understood in more than one way.
14. Is she ________ and arrogant or just shy?
15. Without my glasses, I ________ into the wrong room.
16. I came in and ________ a fire in the stove.
17. She carefully ________ each step of her plan.
18. When heated, the mixture becomes soft and ________ and can be formed by various techniques into a vast array of shapes and sizes.

19. He was famous for his prowess as an athlete.

20. At first she threatened to dismiss me, but later she surmounted relented

21. He mediates a settlement between labor and management.

22. It was always when you most wanted a direct answer that Greenfield came up with a circumlocution

Exercise 5-C 偏难词自测练习 (30 minutes)

Please fill in the blanks, choosing the words from the list. Each word can only be used once. Then you can go back to the Word List and check your answers.
请从表格所列单词中选出与下列中文意思对应的单词，填入空格，每个单词只能使用一次。完毕之后，请回到《SAT巴朗词表：乱序版》中对应的单元，核对答案，并标注自己没有填对的单词。

Word List

fatalism	sectarian	exposure	despot	ratiocination
barricade	faze	imply	pandemonium	annex
chasten	antithesis	physiological	minute	brunt
quorum	stupefy	renown	metamorphosis	chaotic
entitlement	amnesty	disputatious	fledgling	terminology
mores	moribund	ideology	expertise	ambulatory
diversity	impecunious	creed	ecologist	puerile
opus	rescind	title	rebuff	
catalyst	myriad	recurrent	homogeneous	
anthropologist	benevolent	fancy	fundamental	

（拥有某物的）权利；津贴 entitlement　　对比；对立面 antithesis

生态学家 ecologist　　专业知识；专业技术 expertise

作品，杰作 opus　　微小的 minute

匆匆设置的壁垒或路障；障碍（物）barricade　　人类学家 anthropologist

附加；吞并 annex

无数，极大数量；无数的；多种的 myriad

大赦，赦免 amnesty

暗示；意味 imply

名望，声誉 renown

术语 terminology

信条 creed

没有钱的，身无分文的 impecunious

暴君；专制者 despot

惩戒；（通过惩罚而使坏习惯等）改正 chasten

大混乱，喧闹 pandemonium

不同点，多样性 diversity

宿命论 fatalism

想法；一时的兴致；爱好 fancy

回绝，驳斥；断然拒绝 rebuff

变形；变态 metamorphosis

宗派的，派系的；思想狭隘的 sectarian

爱争论的，好辩的 disputatious

所有权；称号，头衔；标题，名称 title

乐善好施的 benevolent

冲击，主要冲力 brunt

垂死的 moribund

推理，推论 ratiocination

思想体系，思想意识 idealogy

法定人数 quorum

基础的，基本的，根本的 fundamental

风俗，习惯；道德观念 mores

使恍惚；使茫然 stupefy

无经验的 fledgling

同种类的，同性质的 homogenous

催化剂 catalyst

能够走动的，不需要卧床的 ambulatory

混乱的 chaotic

使发窘，使惊慌失措 faze

暴露；揭露；公开 exposure

废除，解除，取消 rescind

生理学的 physiological

幼稚的，孩子气的 puerile

复发的，周期性发生的 reccurent

Review: Word List 6

- □ angular
- □ minutiae
- □ verity
- □ lexicon
- □ précis
- □ placid
- □ mammal
- □ accomplice
- □ grudging
- □ ethos
- □ implement
- □ deducible
- □ coercion
- □ pique
- □ discretion
- □ liaison
- □ onus
- □ dissolution
- □ retaliation
- □ witticism
- □ crux
- □ apolitical
- □ metaphor
- □ callow
- □ determination
- □ ineffectual
- □ surrogate
- □ gloat
- □ hyperbole
- □ malicious
- □ stoic
- □ anemia
- □ unanimity
- □ civil
- □ appropriate
- □ dispatch
- □ solitude
- □ reproach
- □ complacency
- □ anomalous
- □ ford
- □ glacial
- □ sardonic
- □ frigid
- □ rancor
- □ betray
- □ deface
- □ pragmatic
- □ terrestrial
- □ prodigy
- □ infallible
- □ exclaim
- □ stratum
- □ tractable
- □ causal
- □ watershed
- □ defection
- □ precipitate
- □ imperative
- □ dilapidated
- □ martial
- □ astronomical
- □ palliate
- □ flabbergasted
- □ conventional
- □ inflated
- □ nascent
- □ formidable
- □ glaring
- □ transport
- □ unaccountable
- □ jovial
- □ coalesce
- □ engaging
- □ apropos
- □ genre
- □ anarchist
- □ avow
- □ topography
- □ foible
- □ psyche
- □ slacken
- □ antiseptic
- □ precedent
- □ submissive
- □ dilettante
- □ consistency
- □ diverse
- □ dearth
- □ withdrawn
- □ blurt
- □ secrete
- □ trifling
- □ empirical
- □ impoverished
- □ enormity
- □ perverse
- □ derelict
- □ asylum
- □ inexorable

Exercise 6

Exercise 6-A Multiple-Choice Quiz (5 minutes)

Please choose the best answer that conveys the meaning of the given word. There is only one correct choice.
请根据所给单词的意思，从A,B,C,D四个选项中找出其同义词，每题只有一个正确答案。

1. verity (*n*)
A. variety
B. penalty
C. truth
D. faith

2. placid (*adj*)
A. considerable
B. decisive
C. solid
D. peaceful

3. implement (*v*)
A. enact
B. comprise
C. plunge
D. divide

4. accomplice (*n*)
A. petty details
B. partner in crime
C. witty saying
D. layer of Earth's surface

5. gloat (*v*)
A. express evil satisfaction
B. cry out suddenly
C. declare openly
D. hide away

6. grudging (*adj*)
A. staggering
B. pragmatic
C. reluctant
D. civil

7. appropriate (*v*)
A. acquire
B. appreciate
C. attach
D. adjust

8. malicious (*adj*)
A. ineffectual
B. angular
C. terrestrial
D. spiteful

9. sardonic (*adj*)
A. satisfied
B. sarcastic
C. secure
D. saturated

10. infallible (*adj*)
A. causal
B. martial
C. unerring
D. astronomical

11. onus (*n*)

A. burden
B. figment
C. metaphor
D. hyperbole

12. precipitate (*adj*)

A. hasty
B. fragile
C. delicious
D. attractive

13. slacken (*v*)

A. lack
B. slake
C. loosen
D. proceed

14. blurt (*v*)

A. utter
B. treat
C. preserve
D. maneuver

15. palliate (*v*)

A. appall
B. parallel
C. alleviate
D. elevate

16. nascent (*adj*)

A. native
B. incipient
C. inflated
D. tractable

17. reproach (*v*)

A. resuscitate
B. repel
C. reiterate
D. rebuke

18. deface (*v*)

A. conjecture
B. depict
C. disfigure
D. innovate

19. betray (*v*)

A. belittle
B. reveal
C. contempt
D. surpass

20. stoic (*adj*)

A. impassive
B. devoid
C. chronic
D. impressive

Exercise 6-B Matching Quiz (5 minutes)

Match the words from the two columns.
从右边列表中选出和左边单词意思匹配的词汇，把它们用线连起来。

Ⓐ

ethos	compulsion
lexicon	substitute
coercion	send
surrogate	self-satisfaction
unanimity	dictionary
dispatch	irregular
complacency	character
anomalous	consensus

Ⓑ

prodigy	genius
formidable	ecstasy
transport	yielding
engaging	irrational
submissive	charming
perverse	difficult

Ⓒ

withdrawn	trivial
dearth	merry
inexorable	scarcity
trifling	introverted
jovial	relentless

Exercise 6-C 偏难词自测练习 (30 minutes)

Please fill in the blanks, choosing the words from the list. Each word can only be used once. Then you can go back to the Word List and check your answers.
请从表格所列单词中选出与下列中文意思对应的单词，填入空格，每个单词只能使用一次。完毕之后，请回到《SAT巴朗词表：乱序版》中对应的单元，核对答案，并标注自己没有填对的单词。

Word List

angular	metaphor	terrestrial	inflated	dilettante
minutiae	callow	exclaim	glaring	consistency
précis	determination	stratum	unaccountable	diverse
mammal	ineffectual	tractable	coalesce	secrete
deducible	hyperbole	causal	apropos	empirical
pique	anemia	watershed	genre	improverished
discretion	civil	defection	anarchist	enormity
liaison	solitude	imperative	avow	derelict
dissolution	ford	dilapidated	topography	asylum
retaliation	glacial	martial	foible	
witticism	frigid	astronomical	psyche	
crux	rancor	flabbergasted	antiseptic	
apolitical	pragmatic	conventional	precedent	

决心；测量；决定 determination

呼喊，惊叫 exclaim

易驾驭的，驯良的 tractable

实际的，注重实效的 pragmatic

关于，有关 apropos

弱点，（性格上的）缺点 foible

寒冷的 frigid

类型，流派，体裁 genre

大纲，摘要 précis

巨大的 astronomical

抛弃的；玩忽职守的，疏忽的；废弃物，弃船 derelict

关键点 crux

孤独，独居 solitude

（修辞）夸张法 hyperbole

夸张的，膨胀的 inflated

报复，报仇 retaliation

公民的，民间的；有礼貌的 civil

（艺术、科学等方面）半吊子；业余爱好者 dilettante

合作，交流；私通 liaison

防腐剂，杀菌剂 antiseptic

惯例；先例 precedent

深仇，怨恨 rancor

战争的，军事的 martial

不悦，生气；激起；使生气 pique

无法解释的；莫名其妙的，不可理解的 unaccountable

分水岭，转折点 watershed

有角的；固执的，死板的 angular

不同的，各种各样的 diverse

显眼的，耀眼的 glaring

无效的；不成功的 ineffectual

公开宣布 avow

（修辞）暗喻 metaphor

贫困的，赤贫的 impoverished

可推断的 deducible

年轻而无经验的；未成熟的 callow

必要的，势在必行的；极重要的；需要；imperative

命令 imperative

谨慎；决定能力 discretion

大吃一惊的，目瞪口呆的 flabbergasted

避难所；庇护 asylum

常规的，惯例的 conventional

一致性；连贯性；浓度 consistency

因果关系的 causal

陆地的，陆生的，地球上的 terrestial

微小的细节 minutiae

无政府主义者；主张废弃权威者

anarchist

地层；社会阶层 stratum

结合；熔合 coalesce

冰的，冰冷的 glacial

叛逃，变节 defection

不关心政治的 apolitical

隐藏，隐匿；分泌 secrete

哺乳动物 mammal

荒废的，破坏的 dilapidated

地质，地形 topography

妙语，俏皮话 witticism

贫血 anemia

心智，心灵 psyche

经验主义的 empirical

浅滩 ford

（问题、后果等的）巨大，艰巨 enormity

瓦解；消散；解除 dissolution

Review: Word List 7

- □ indiscriminate
- □ salient
- □ onerous
- □ approbation
- □ ethnic
- □ acoustics
- □ grievance
- □ fortuitous
- □ catharsis
- □ agnostic
- □ atrophy
- □ futile
- □ barren
- □ camouflage
- □ hypocritical
- □ criterion
- □ hybrid
- □ imperceptible
- □ humane
- □ denounce
- □ inconsequential
- □ anthology
- □ confrontation
- □ prompt
- □ cavil
- □ dormant
- □ fluctuate
- □ burlesque
- □ blighted
- □ arbitrator
- □ adorn
- □ affected
- □ archaic
- □ foreboding
- □ generality
- □ protocol
- □ engender
- □ abbreviate
- □ partition
- □ guise
- □ apparatus
- □ surpass
- □ graphic
- □ disapprobation
- □ punitive
- □ unprecedented
- □ attrition
- □ founder
- □ disavowal
- □ impetus
- □ enumerate
- □ indigent
- □ inequity
- □ inaugurate
- □ severity
- □ downcast
- □ offensive
- □ absolve
- □ adversity
- □ vital
- □ implicate
- □ attest
- □ advocacy
- □ ostracize
- □ eloquence
- □ pecuniary
- □ heinous
- □ stem
- □ consolidation
- □ anguish
- □ congenital
- □ beam
- □ check
- □ irrevocable
- □ compute
- □ nurture
- □ repertoire
- □ posthumous
- □ derivative
- □ hypothetical
- □ perfunctory
- □ sophomoric
- □ peruse
- □ booming
- □ methodical
- □ apprenticeship
- □ predispose
- □ loquacious
- □ amorphous
- □ fraudulent
- □ rigorous
- □ exuberance
- □ reimburse
- □ quail
- □ esteem
- □ unpalatable
- □ decrepit
- □ willful
- □ pall
- □ transmute

Exercise 7

Exercise 7-A Multiple-Choice Quiz (5 minutes)

Please choose the best answer that conveys the meaning of the given word. There is only one correct choice.
请根据所给单词的意思，从A,B,C,D四个选项中找出其同义词，每题只有一个正确答案。

1. salient (*adj*)
   A. striking
   B. ethnic
   C. hybrid
   D. benevolent

2. inconsequential (*adj*)
   A. orderly
   B. insignificant
   C. impossible
   D. dormant

3. grievance (*n*)
   A. advocacy
   B. apprenticeship
   C. complaint
   D. grave

4. denounce (*v*)
   A. prompt
   B. fluctuate
   C. abbreviate
   D. condemn

5. punitive (*adj*)
   A. offensive
   B. punishing
   C. vital
   D. hypothetical

6. absolve (*v*)
   A. implicate
   B. founder
   C. pardon
   D. compute

7. stem (*v*)
   A. check
   B. nurture
   C. esteem
   D. sculpt

8. pecuniary (*adj*)
   A. affected
   B. financial
   C. willful
   D. rigorous

9. reimburse (*v*)
   A. repay
   B. retreat
   C. reproach
   D. resemble

10. ostracize (*v*)
   A. contemplate
   B. exceed
   C. exclude
   D. distribute

11. inaugurate (*v*)

A. innovate
B. engulf
C. initiate
D. embody

12. enumerate (*v*)

A. excavate
B. economize
C. list
D. distinguish

13. indigent (*adj*)

A. impoverished
B. deficient
C. indignant
D. indefatigable

14. blighted (*adj*)

A. prevailing
B. distinct
C. facial
D. destroyed

15. imperceptible (*adj*)

A. unimportant
B. undetectable
C. illegible
D. disagreeable

16. onerous (*adj*)

A. hypercritical
B. graphic
C. burdensome
D. indiscriminate

17. fortuitous (*adj*)

A. fortunate
B. sterile
C. immense
D. accidental

18. futile (*adj*)

A. premature
B. useless
C. energetic
D. overcast

19. camouflage (*v*)

A. conceal
B. impel
C. convey
D. omit

20. inequity (*n*)

A. apparatus
B. catharsis
C. veneration
D. unfairness

21. heinous (*adj*)

A. unprecedented
B. barren
C. evil
D. acoustic

Exercise 7-B Sentence-Completion Quiz (30 minutes)

Please fill in the blanks, choosing the words from the list. Each word can only be used once.
请从表格所列单词中选出最符合语境的单词，填入空格，每个单词只能使用一次。

Word List

quail	congenital	engender	anthology	irrevocable
criterion	adorn	partition	fraudulent	loquacious
archaic	beam	atrophy	posthumous	
decrepit	peruse	attest	predispose	
consolidation	derivative	foreboding	adversity	

1. The ________ of the country into two parts caused many problems.
2. An ability may ________ if it is not used.
3. Police records ________ to his long history of violence.
4. When John was 17, he died of ________ heart disease.
5. His good manners ________ people to like him.
6. ________ makes a man wise, not rich.
7. The waitress ________ a cheerful welcome to the guests.
8. We ________ the company's financial statements for the past five years.
9. A number of critics found the film ________ and predictable.
10. This is a ________ lawsuit brought by a convicted felon, and we look forward to defending it in court.
11. Michael Jackson's second ________ album *X-scape* is soon to be released worldwide. The first album released after his death in 2009 was poorly received.
12. The coward ________ before the enemy.
13. The young girl ________ herself with jewels.
14. The normally ________ Mr. O'Reilly has said little.
15. Hatred ________ violence.
16. The most important ________ for entry is that applicants must design and make their own work.
17. The company does some things in ________ ways, such as not using computers for bookkeeping.

18. I shall post this letter on my arrival. I shall not come back. My decision is irrevocable.

19. Dark blues may be foreboding or an indication of worry or fear.

20. An anthology is a collection of writings by different writers published together in one book.

21. The film had been shot in a posthumous decrepit old police station.

22. The consolidation and emergence of local newspaper monopolies, also promoted impartiality.

Exercise 7-C 偏难词自测练习 (30 minutes)

Please fill in the blanks, choosing the words from the list. Each word can only be used once. Then you can go back to the Word List and check your answers.

请从表格所列单词中选出与下列中文意思对应的单词，填入空格，每个单词只能使用一次。完毕之后，请回到《SAT巴朗词表：乱序版》中对应的单元，核对答案，并标注自己没有填对的单词。

indiscriminate	cavil	graphic	advocacy	apprenticeship
approbation	dormant	disapprobation	eloquence	amorphous
ethnic	fluctuate	unprecedented	anguish	rigorous
acoustics	burlesque	attrition	check	exuberance
catharsis	arbitrator	founder	compute	esteem
agnostic	affected	disavowal	nurture	unpalatable
barren	generality	impetus	repertoire	willful
hypocritical	protocol	severity	hypothetical	pall
hybrid	abbreviate	downcast	perfunctory	transmute
humane	guise	offensive	sophomoric	
confrontation	apparatus	vital	booming	
prompt	surpass	implicate	methodical	

声学；音响效果 acoustic

杂种；混血儿；混合物；混合的；杂种的 hybrid

严肃，严格，严重 severity

生机勃勃的，重大的，生命的 vital

通则，概论 generality

器械，设备 apparatus

停止；抑制，遏制 check

不加选择的；杂乱无章的，混乱的 indiscriminate

外观；装束 guise

（准备好演出的）节目单 repertoire

提示，促使；（给演员）提白 prompt

养育，教养，培养 nurture

不以为然；非难 disapprobation

学徒年限 apprenticeship

模仿嘲弄 burlesque

敷衍的，例行的 perfunctory

推动力，促进，冲力 impetus

故意的；固执的，任性的 willful

空前的，没有先例的 unprecedented

贫瘠的；不结果实的；缺乏的 barren

假装的，做作的 affected

种族的 ethnic

仁慈的，人道的 humane

攻击的，无礼的，讨厌的 offensive

宣泄；通便 catharsis

伪善的；矫饰的 hypocritical

支持，拥护 advocacy

能言善辩 eloquence

挑剔，吹毛求疵 cavit

无组织的，无定形的 amorphous

睡着的；休眠的，蛰伏的 dormant

严格的，严厉的，严酷的 rigorous

味道差的；令人不快的 unpalatable

假定的，基于假设的 hypothetical

消耗；人员自然缩减；磨损 attrition

公断人 arbitrator

一知半解的 sophomoric

尊敬，敬重 esteem

面对；对抗 confrontation

草案，协议 protocal

超越，胜过 surpass

沮丧的，悲哀的 downcast

批准，认可 approbation

缩短，缩略 abbreviate

使牵连其中；暗示 implicate

计算，估算 compute

不可知论者 agnostic

图解的；描写生动的 graphic

否认，不承认 disavowal

剧痛；极度的痛苦 anguish

波动；变动 fluctuate

失败；沉没；创建者，缔造者 founder

系统的 methodical

变得平淡、乏味 pall

丰富，茂盛；热情洋溢；精神焕发 exubergance

使变形；使变质 transmute

低沉有回响的；繁荣的 booming

Review: Word List 8

- □ philistine
- □ valedictory
- □ paradox
- □ compact
- □ aesthetic
- □ exhort
- □ propitious
- □ prone
- □ fret
- □ viable
- □ constraint
- □ transition
- □ zeal
- □ outstrip
- □ dire
- □ ultimate
- □ equitable
- □ circumspect
- □ demean
- □ demur
- □ turmoil
- □ intimacy
- □ quarry
- □ arbiter
- □ penchant
- □ credulity
- □ stipulate
- □ liberator
- □ figment
- □ prune
- □ imponderable
- □ denizen
- □ remnant
- □ mollify
- □ forensic
- □ servile
- □ orthodox
- □ industrious
- □ heresy
- □ arable
- □ insurgent
- □ affirmation
- □ grueling
- □ terse
- □ categorical
- □ egregious
- □ accelerate
- □ protrude
- □ abet
- □ mobile
- □ sanction
- □ exemplary
- □ theoretical
- □ vernacular
- □ atypical
- □ meditation
- □ flair
- □ temporize
- □ resentment
- □ proliferation
- □ indeterminate
- □ impel
- □ coincidence
- □ bigotry
- □ predicament
- □ embargo
- □ besiege
- □ repellent
- □ permeable
- □ foil
- □ capricious
- □ negligence
- □ bizarre
- □ instigate
- □ tenet
- □ sedate
- □ mystify
- □ efficacy
- □ chameleon
- □ contract
- □ thespian
- □ impede
- □ credence
- □ summation
- □ circumvent
- □ stringent
- □ voluble
- □ petulant
- □ aberrant
- □ abominable
- □ obtuse
- □ partisan
- □ manifest
- □ optional
- □ connivance
- □ invigorate
- □ conciliatory
- □ auxiliary
- □ infer
- □ prolific

Exercise 8

Exercise 8-A Multiple-Choice Quiz (5 minutes)

Please choose the best answer that conveys the meaning of the given word. There is only one correct choice.
请根据所给单词的意思，从A,B,C,D四个选项中找出其同义词，每题只有一个正确答案。

1. paradox (*n*)
A. proxy
B. contradiction
C. discretion
D. affirmation

2. egregious (*adj*)
A. ultimate
B. mobile
C. permeable
D. shocking

3. exhort (*v*)
A. intrigue
B. extinguish
C. urge
D. drain

4. predicament (*n*)
A. accretion
B. coincidence
C. dilemma
D. efficacy

5. foil (*v*)
A. frustrate
B. ominous
C. mystify
D. impel

6. sedate (*adj*)
A. stern
B. optional
C. atypical
D. composed

7. besiege (*v*)
A. infer
B. beset
C. betray
D. strength

8. capricious (*adj*)
A. timid
B. durable
C. nutritious
D. unpredictable

9. aesthetic (*adj*)
A. artistic
B. considerate
C. substantial
D. complicated

10. terse (*adj*)
A. urban
B. ritual
C. vertical
D. compact

11. viable (*adj*)
A. obvious
B. practical
C. excellent
D. convenient

12. turmoil (*n*)
A. quarry
B. intimacy
C. transition
D. commotion

13. servile (*adj*)
A. prone
B. interior
C. subservient
D. marine

14. outstrip (*v*)
A. accelerate
B. impede
C. oust
D. outdo

15. mollify (*v*)
A. soothe
B. ascend
C. evaporate
D. dizzy

16. sanction (*v*)
A. approve
B. sacrifice
C. apprehend
D. split

17. voluble (*adj*)
A. extrinsic
B. talkative
C. rhetorical
D. ephemeral

18. exemplary (*adj*)
A. innovative
B. rational
C. outstanding
D. loathsome

19. fret (*v*)
A. worry
B. grant
C. recommend
D. pose

20. demean (*v*)
A. revise
B. construct
C. humiliate
D. stamp

21. prune (*v*)
A. unravel
B. despair
C. provoke
D. diminish

22. prolific (*adj*)
A. bulky
B. fruitful
C. refined
D. subtle

Exercise 8-B Matching Quiz (5 minutes)

Match the words from the two columns.
从右边列表中选出和左边单词意思匹配的词汇，把它们用线连起来。

A

dire	delay
propitious	disastrous
remnant	talent
temporize	rigid
flair	favorable
theoretical	hypothetical
stringent	remainder

B

zeal	cultivatable
equitable	rebellious
stipulate	impartial
demur	absolute
industrious	specify
arable	indignation
categorical	enthusiasm
insurgent	object
resentment	evident
manifest	diligent

C

conciliatory	energize
invigorate	growth
bizarre	compulsion
proliferation	reconciling
constraint	peculiar

Exercise 8-C 偏难词自测练习 (30 minutes)

Please fill in the blanks, choosing the words from the list. Each word can only be used once. Then you can go back to the Word List and check your answers.
请从表格所列单词中选出与下列中文意思对应的单词，填入空格，每个单词只能使用一次。完毕之后，请回到《SAT巴朗词表：乱序版》中对应的单元，核对答案，并标注自己没有填对的单词。

Word List

philistine	liberator	mobile	instigate	aberrant
valedictory	figment	vernacular	tenet	abominable
compact	imponderable	atypical	mystify	obtuse
prone	denizen	meditation	efficacy	partisan
transition	forensic	indeterminate	chameleon	optional
ultimate	orthodox	impel	contract	connivance
circumspect	heresy	coincidence	thespian	auxiliary
intimacy	affirmation	bigotry	impede	infer
quarry	grueling	embargo	credence	
arbiter	accelerate	repellent	summation	
penchant	protrude	permeable	circumvent	
credulity	abet	negligence	petulant	

有…倾向的，易于…的 prone

疏忽，粗心大意 negligence

过渡 transition

日常用语，白话 vernacular

平庸的人，没有文化修养的人；市侩的人 philistine

排斥的；令人反感的 repellent

沉思，冥想 meditation

蒙蔽，迷惑 mystify

小心的，慎重的 circumspect

传统的，正统的 orthodox

猎物，追求目标 quarry

妨碍；拖延 impede

脾气坏的 petulant

变色龙 chameleon

嗜好，爱好 penchant

推动，驱使 impel

共谋；纵容；默许 connivance

断言，肯定；（法庭）证词 affirmation

钝的，不锋利的；愚笨的 obtuse

可移动的，不固定的 mobile

告别的，告辞的 valedictory

教唆（犯罪）；煽动 abet

贸易禁令，禁运 embargo

无法精确估量的 imponderable

适于法庭的，公开辩论的 forensic

智取；包围 circumvent

最后的，终极的 ultimate

信任 credence

加速 accelerate

解放者，释放者 liberator

折磨的，使筋疲力尽的 grueling

仲裁人，裁决人 aribiter

随意的，可选择的 optional

收缩；订约；感染 contract

讨厌的，令人憎恶的；极坏的 abominable
巧合 coincidence
辅助的 auxiliary
戏剧的 thespian
居民；常客，老主顾 denizen
可穿透的，可渗透的 permeable
激起，怂恿，煽动 instigate
合计；总结 summation
契约；合同；挤满的，紧密的；坚实的；简洁的 compact
信条，原则 tenet
突出 protrude
非典型的，反常的 atypical
臆造的事物，虚构的事 figment
亲密，隐私，亲昵行为 intimacy
有效性，功效 efficacy
异端邪说，异教 heresy
异常的，脱轨的 aberrant
不确定的，不明的，模糊的 indeterminate
偏袒的；党派的 partisan
轻信，易受骗 credulity
推断，推论出 infer
固执，顽固 bigotry

Review: Word List 9

- □ transparent
- □ amplify
- □ delete
- □ amiable
- □ flippant
- □ exigency
- □ scrupulous
- □ piety
- □ encumber
- □ heterodox
- □ autocratic
- □ berate
- □ exacerbate
- □ vapid
- □ bourgeois
- □ cosmopolitan
- □ pomposity
- □ retrieve
- □ lackluster
- □ dissimulate
- □ blasé
- □ recipient
- □ clique
- □ shun
- □ virulent
- □ censor
- □ innate
- □ facilitate
- □ assail
- □ benefactor
- □ feral
- □ equivocal
- □ execrable
- □ faction
- □ obnoxious
- □ verge
- □ trenchant
- □ delineate
- □ agent
- □ comparable
- □ diminution
- □ qualms
- □ rudimentary
- □ embody
- □ recession
- □ pathos
- □ assumption
- □ presentiment
- □ prerogative
- □ sophistry
- □ rigor
- □ incidental
- □ plagiarize
- □ inane
- □ suavity
- □ coddle
- □ aftermath
- □ archive
- □ imminent
- □ thrive
- □ provident
- □ parody
- □ justification
- □ abstinence
- □ partiality
- □ odyssey
- □ bicker
- □ advent
- □ affinity
- □ insolvent
- □ insularity
- □ retrospective
- □ enduring
- □ dispassionate
- □ incongruous
- □ yield
- □ revoke
- □ haughtiness
- □ maxim
- □ controvert
- □ dismiss
- □ ostensible
- □ disparate
- □ garrulous
- □ erudite
- □ inclined
- □ indicative
- □ proponent
- □ evocative
- □ soluble
- □ intrepid
- □ aptitude
- □ plausible
- □ acumen
- □ abstain
- □ lax
- □ proletarian
- □ mendacious
- □ orient
- □ renovate

Exercise 9

Exercise 9-A Multiple-Choice Quiz (5 minutes)

Please choose the best answer that conveys the meaning of the given word. There is only one correct choice.
请根据所给单词的意思，从A,B,C,D四个选项中找出其同义词，每题只有一个正确答案。

1. scrupulous (*adj*)
   A. rudimentary
   B. inclined
   C. meticulous
   D. expansive

2. autocratic (*adj*)
   A. dictatorial
   B. indicative
   C. soluble
   D. profitable

3. diminution (*n*)
   A. agent
   B. advent
   C. yield
   D. reduction

4. insolvent (*adj*)
   A. enduring
   B. plausible
   C. drastic
   D. bankrupt

5. exacerbate (*v*)
   A. amplify
   B. embody
   C. thrive
   D. compound

6. dismiss (*v*)
   A. reject
   B. inflame
   C. orient
   D. circulate

7. assail (*v*)
   A. attack
   B. assess
   C. assign
   D. assimilate

8. dissimulate (*v*)
   A. deposit
   B. pretend
   C. disseminate
   D. dispute

9. shun (*v*)
   A. shrink
   B. evade
   C. preside
   D. inherit

10. encumber (*v*)
    A. assemble
    B. symbolize
    C. impede
    D. compensate

11. vapid (*adj*)
A. comparable
B. dominant
C. dreary
D. chronic

12. equivocal (*adj*)
A. ambiguous
B. ambitious
C. equitable
D. lighthearted

13. incidental (*adj*)
A. perceptual
B. non-essential
C. transparent
D. valid

14. garrulous (*adj*)
A. conservative
B. tricky
C. inviting
D. voluble

15. incongruous (*adj*)
A. inappropriate
B. ingenuous
C. incoherent
D. inherent

16. erudite (*adj*)
A. honorable
B. considerate
C. mur
D. scholarly

17. retrieve (*v*)
A. revoke
B. refute
C. reiterate
D. recover

18. haughtiness (*n*)
A. rigor
B. arrogance
C. significance
D. potential

19. inane (*adj*)
A. innate
B. artistical
C. silly
D. meaningful

Exercise 9-B Sentence-Completion Quiz (30 minutes)

Please fill in the blanks, choosing the words from the list. Each word can only be used once.
请从表格所列单词中选出最符合语境的单词，填入空格，每个单词只能使用一次。

Word List

plagiarize	mendacious	parody	justification	imminent
recession	acumen	maxim	lax	partiality
pathos	aftermath	aptitude	amiable	
exigency	renovate	provident	evocative	
ostensible	disparate	flippant	cosmopolitan	

1. The family is rich, and extremely sophisticated and ________.
2. ________ is a quality in a situation, film, or play that makes people feel sadness and pity.
3. The ________ of a situation are the demands or difficulties that you have to deal with as part of it.
4. A ________ is a humorous piece of writing, drama, or music that imitates the style of a well-known person or represents a familiar situation in an exaggerated way.
5. She is an ________ girl and gets along with everyone in the office.
6. The taste of the cakes was ________ of my childhood.
7. Don't be ________! This is serious!
8. His ________ purpose was charity, but his real goal was popularity.
9. A ________ person is someone who tells lies.
10. ________ is the ability to make good judgments and quick decisions.
11. He had a ________ for chess.
12. He is ________ of his money.
13. Half the ideas in his talk were ________ from an article I wrote last month.
14. That's because the country was in a severe auto motor ________ under depression.
15. I believe the ________ that actions speak louder than words.
16. Someone's ________ for a particular kind of work or activity is their ability to learn it quickly and to do it well.
17. Something ________ means it is almost certain to happen very soon.
18. The couple spent thousands ________ the house.
19. Chalk and cheese are ________ substances.
20. ________ security allowed the thieves to enter.
21. A ________ for something is an acceptable reason or explanation for it.
22. It stems from the states' dire fiscal straits in the ________ of the recession.

Exercise 9-C 偏难词自测练习 (30 minutes)

Please fill in the blanks, choosing the words from the list. Each word can only be used once. Then you can go back to the Word List and check your answers.

请从表格所列单词中选出与下列中文意思对应的单词，填入空格，每个单词只能使用一次。完毕之后，请回到《SAT巴朗词表：乱序版》中对应的单元，核对答案，并标注自己没有填对的单词。

Word List

transparent	*virulent*	*agent*	*archive*	*revoke*
amplify	*censor*	*comparable*	*thrive*	*controvert*
delete	*innate*	*qualms*	*abstinence*	*inclined*
piety	*facilitate*	*rudimentary*	*odyssey*	*indicative*
heterodox	*benefactor*	*embody*	*bicker*	*proponent*
berate	*feral*	*assumption*	*advent*	*soluble*
bourgeois	*execrable*	*presentiment*	*affinity*	*intrepid*
pomposity	*faction*	*prerogative*	*insularity*	*plausible*
lackluster	*obnoxious*	*sophistry*	*retrospective*	*abstain*
blasé	*verge*	*rigor*	*enduring*	*proletarian*
recipient	*trenchant*	*suavity*	*dispassionate*	*orient*
clique	*delineate*	*coddle*	*yield*	

虔诚，虔敬 piety	严格，严酷 rigor
边缘，界限 verge	先天的，天生的 innate
类似的 comparable	投降，屈服 yield
小集团，派系 clique	放大；增强 amplify
假设；承担，担任 assumption	倾向的；倾斜的 inclined
担忧，不安，良心责备 qualms	有助于，使容易 facilitate
使人讨厌的，可憎的 obnoxious	支持者；拥护者 proponent
兴旺，繁荣 thrive	似乎是真的，貌似有道理的；华而不实的 plausible
中产阶级；渴求名利的；平庸的 bourgeois	妄自尊大 pomposity
特权；毋庸置疑的权利 prerogative	出现，到来 advent

极坏的，极差的 execrable
非正统的，异端的 heterodox
长途的冒险旅行 odyssey
预感 presentiment
派别；小团体；派系斗争 faction
描绘，描写，勾勒 delineate
痛斥，严责 berate
节制，节食，戒酒 abstinence
未充分发展的；基本的；初步的 rudimentary
温和；文雅 suavity
厌倦于享乐的 blasé
撤回，废除；吊销 revoke
诡辩 sophistry
回顾的 retrospective
可溶解的；可解决的 soluble
划掉，删掉 delete
反驳，驳斥 controvert
无畏的，勇猛的 intrepid
捐助者；赞助人 benefactor
无产者，工人 proletarian
审查员 censor
体现（思想，原则等）；包括，收录 embody
剧毒的；恶毒的，充满敌意的 virulent
有力的，有效的；刻薄的，锋利的 trenchant
档案；档案室 archive
接受者 recipient
斗嘴 bicker
媒介；代理人；执行官 agent
持久的，持续的 enduring
显然的，明晰的；透明的 transparent
（思想、观点等的）偏狭；与外界隔绝 insularity
冷静的；不带偏见的 dispassionate
（动物）野生的 feral
死气沉沉的 lackluster
密切关系 affinity
暗示的，预示的 indicative
自制，戒除 abstain
给…定方向；使适应 orient
溺爱 coddle

Review: Word List 10

- □ discord
- □ vignette
- □ august
- □ perpetuate
- □ subsidiary
- □ cataclysm
- □ conjure
- □ feasible
- □ relic
- □ reserve
- □ voluminous
- □ static
- □ frugality
- □ outwit
- □ epitome
- □ colossal
- □ withhold
- □ interrogate
- □ artifact
- □ compromise
- □ idiom
- □ qualified
- □ rhetoric
- □ gainsay
- □ quaint
- □ cogitate
- □ sagacious
- □ avalanche
- □ disinterested
- □ grapple
- □ oscillate
- □ magnanimous
- □ impunity
- □ log
- □ nepotism
- □ convoluted
- □ flagrant
- □ circuitous
- □ obsessive
- □ pathological
- □ encipher
- □ asymmetric
- □ adversary
- □ recount
- □ feint
- □ bountiful
- □ bemused
- □ acuity
- □ relish
- □ expansive
- □ bravado
- □ exempt
- □ expenditure
- □ wake
- □ cerebral
- □ condense
- □ quizzical
- □ fidelity
- □ stipend
- □ eccentric
- □ pore
- □ malignant
- □ fastidious
- □ constituent
- □ inimical
- □ pliant
- □ extraneous
- □ lackadaisical
- □ ruse
- □ summit
- □ culminate
- □ denigrate
- □ mundane
- □ paraphernalia
- □ illusion
- □ menial
- □ deleterious
- □ allusion
- □ residue
- □ beguile
- □ frustrate
- □ sedition
- □ aloft
- □ fugitive
- □ solicitous
- □ bluster
- □ lucrative
- □ caption
- □ attenuate
- □ affliction
- □ reparable
- □ solvent
- □ zealot
- □ adherent
- □ quell
- □ panoramic
- □ pacify
- □ chicanery
- □ precarious
- □ abstruse

Exercise 10

Exercise 10-A Multiple-Choice Quiz (5 minutes)

Please choose the best answer that conveys the meaning of the given word. There is only one correct choice.
请根据所给单词的意思，从A,B,C,D四个选项中找出其同义词，每题只有一个正确答案。

1. frugality (*n*)
A. affection
B. presumption
C. symptom
D. economy

2. feasible (*adj*)
A. commercial
B. representative
C. practical
D. frantic

3. perpetuate (*v*)
A. eternalize
B. purchase
C. motivate
D. incorporate

4. adversary (*n*)
A. opponent
B. spectacle
C. transfiguration
D. rhetoric

5. beguile (*v*)
A. outwit
B. deceive
C. adorn
D. possess

6. deleterious (*adj*)
A. sluggish
B. solvent
C. inimical
D. asymmetric

7. oscillate (*v*)
A. fluctuate
B. reserve
C. recount
D. discard

8. fastidious (*adj*)
A. rapid
B. principal
C. meticulous
D. eminent

9. precarious (*adj*)
A. reverential
B. intense
C. simplistic
D. hazardous

10. qualified (*adj*)
A. artificial
B. limited
C. beneficial
D. urgent

11. flagrant (*adj*)

A. outrageous
B. superior
C. inferior
D. fragmentary

12. abstruse (*adj*)

A. altruistic
B. extensive
C. decisive
D. obscure

13. mundane (*adj*)

A. genuine
B. acute
C. ordinary
D. maritime

14. static (*adj*)

A. excellent
B. unchanging
C. delicate
D. susceptible

15. gainsay (*v*)

A. deny
B. predict
C. retain
D. inflate

16. extraneous (*adj*)

A. obligatory
B. trivial
C. critical
D. irrelevant

17. lucrative (*adj*)

A. profitable
B. merciful
C. brimful
D. abnormal

18. quell (*v*)

A. dispatch
B. contribute
C. extinguish
D. symbolize

19. pacify (*v*)

A. rectify
B. adjust
C. amplify
D. tranquilize

20. solicitous (*adj*)

A. periodical
B. customary
C. concerned
D. elegant

Exercise 10-B Matching Quiz (5 minutes)

Match the words from the two columns.
从右边列表中选出和左边单词意思匹配的词汇，把它们用线连起来。

A

relic	*abundant*
relish	*remains*
expansive	*impartial*
obsessive	*endanger*
bountiful	*enjoy*
compromise	*eccentric*
sagacious	*addictive*
quaint	*sociable*
disinterested	*shrewd*

B

colossal	*upheaval*
affliction	*conceal*
menial	*immense*
withhold	*pardon*
cataclysm	*distress*
impunity	*lowly*

C

voluminous	*teasing*
convoluted	*capacious*
pliant	*insubordination*
quizzical	*climax*
malignant	*injurious*
culminate	*deferential*
sedition	*intricate*

Exercise 10-C 偏难词自测练习 (30 minutes)

Please fill in the blanks, choosing the words from the list. Each word can only be used once. Then you can go back to the Word List and check your answers.
请从表格所列单词中选出与下列中文意思对应的单词，填入空格，每个单词只能使用一次。完毕之后，请回到《SAT巴朗词表：乱序版》中对应的单元，核对答案，并标注自己没有填对的单词。

Word List

discord	cogitate	bemused	constituent	fugitive
vignette	avalanche	acuity	inimical	bluster
august	grapple	bravado	lackadaisical	caption
subsidiary	magnanimous	exempt	ruse	attenuate
conjure	log	expenditure	summit	reparable
reserve	nepotism	wake	denigrate	solvent
outwit	circuitous	cerebral	paraphernalia	zealot
epitome	pathological	condense	illusion	adherent
interrogate	encipher	fidelity	allusion	panoramic
artifact	asymmetric	stipend	residue	chicanery
idiom	recount	eccentric	frustrate	
rhetoric	feint	pore	aloft	

保守；矜持 reserve

裙带关系，任人唯亲 nepotism

习语，成语；风格，特色 idiom

尖锐，敏锐 acuity

诡计；欺骗 chicanery

典范，典型 epitome

佯攻；移位；虚晃 feint

深思，慎重考虑 cogitate

随身用具，设备 paraphernalia

提及，暗示 allusion

选民，选举人 constituent

（航行）日志 log

诋毁，抹黑 denigrate

钻研，深思，细阅 pore

在高处，在上空 aloft

威严的，宏伟的 august

可修缮的，可补救的 reparable

薪水，薪俸 stipend

懒洋洋的；懒散的，散漫的 lackadaisical

标题；字幕 caption

宽宏大量的，有雅量的 magnanimous

修辞学；花言巧语 rhetoric

雪崩 avalanche

不协调，冲突 discord

不对称的 asymmetric

病理学的；疾病的，病态的 pathological

（船的）尾波；痕迹 wake

格斗，扭打 grapple

虚张声势，逞能 bravado

详细叙述；重新计算 recount

小插图；小品文 vignette

挫败，阻挠 frustrate

被豁免的 exempt

忠实 fidelity

不合常规的；怪异的，古怪的 eccentric

召唤；变戏法；想象 conjure

计谋；策略 ruse

使变细，使变瘦；削弱 attenuate

追随者，拥护者 adherent

人工制品 artifact

迂回的，绕行的 circuitous

把（电文等）译成密码 encipher

困惑的；发呆的 bemused

智胜，骗取 outwit

大脑的；理智的 cerebral

充满敌意的；有害的，不利的 inimical

咆哮；吓唬，胁迫；怒号；吓唬 bluster

开支，支出（额）；产出 expenditure

浓缩，精简 condense

短暂的；流浪的 fugitive

错觉，假象 illusion

询问；审问 interrogate

全景的 panoramic

顶点，顶峰 summit

狂热者 zealot

残余，渣滓；剩余遗产 residue

附属物，（尤指）附属公司；补充物 subsidiar

有偿付能力的；溶剂 solvent

Review: Word List 11

- □ unfathomable
- □ alimony
- □ defame
- □ ample
- □ negligible
- □ intuition
- □ resumption
- □ gloss over
- □ problematic
- □ inconsistency
- □ complement
- □ ambivalence
- □ platitude
- □ vacillate
- □ perceptive
- □ onset
- □ prod
- □ regimen
- □ vantage
- □ bulwark
- □ resurge
- □ gratify
- □ defuse
- □ unwitting
- □ miserly
- □ unkempt
- □ adamant
- □ discerning
- □ import
- □ whimsical
- □ ensconce
- □ jocular
- □ migratory
- □ abstemious
- □ disarray
- □ nebulous
- □ misdemeanor
- □ oblivion
- □ remission
- □ remonstrance
- □ warrant
- □ ramble
- □ unwieldy
- □ replica
- □ universal
- □ incompatible
- □ encroachment
- □ despise
- □ hackneyed
- □ forgo
- □ innovation
- □ decipher
- □ credibility
- □ insurmountable
- □ microcosm
- □ resilient
- □ predecessor
- □ stagnant
- □ poignancy
- □ interminable
- □ cipher
- □ proselytize
- □ overbearing
- □ vindictive
- □ uproarious
- □ agility
- □ abstract
- □ sparse
- □ component
- □ pervasive
- □ abortive
- □ requisite
- □ malevolent
- □ susceptible
- □ sedentary
- □ valid
- □ obstinate
- □ ubiquitous
- □ subsidy
- □ postulate
- □ addiction
- □ aquatic
- □ clemency
- □ reprieve
- □ pliable
- □ symmetry
- □ abrasive
- □ cacophonous
- □ authenticate
- □ conception
- □ unravel
- □ miscellany
- □ quarantine
- □ ascertain
- □ singular
- □ opulence
- □ deposition
- □ retain
- □ militant
- □ quiescent

Exercise 11

Exercise 11-A Multiple-Choice Quiz (5 minutes)

Please choose the best answer that conveys the meaning of the given word. There is only one correct choice.
请根据所给单词的意思，从A,B,C,D四个选项中找出其同义词，每题只有一个正确答案。

1. miserly (*adj*)
   A. abstract
   B. migratory
   C. mean
   D. enormous

2. pervasive (*adj*)
   A. fantastic
   B. dramatic
   C. exclusive
   D. commonplace

3. oblivion (*n*)
   A. forgetfulness
   B. welfare
   C. legislation
   D. implement

4. remission (*n*)
   A. innovation
   B. reprieve
   C. predecessor
   D. component

5. gratify (*v*)
   A. please
   B. alienate
   C. intensify
   D. affront

6. abstemious (*adj*)
   A. universal
   B. sparse
   C. temperate
   D. sedimentary

7. defame (*v*)
   A. collapse
   B. embody
   C. malign
   D. disperse

8. vacillate (*v*)
   A. guarantee
   B. portray
   C. frown
   D. hesitate

9. discerning (*adj*)
   A. stiff
   B. perceptive
   C. dynamic
   D. metabolic

10. warrant (*v*)
    A. retain
    B. digest
    C. procure
    D. justify

11. forgo (*v*)
A. illuminate
B. forage
C. waive
D. define

12. despise (*v*)
A. scorn
B. oblige
C. ratify
D. accrete

13. defuse (*v*)
A. dismiss
B. calculate
C. relieve
D. soak

14. whimsical (*adj*)
A. wretched
B. capricious
C. infallible
D. customary

15. hackneyed (*adj*)
A. fluid
B. technical
C. prestigious
D. commonplace

16. stagnant (*adj*)
A. coarse
B. laden
C. idle
D. static

17. sedentary (*adj*)
A. indispensable
B. unfeigned
C. seated
D. concrete

18. obstinate (*adj*)
A. stubborn
B. aquatic
C. valid
D. singular

19. ramble (*v*)
A. wander
B. rely
C. refine
D. formalize

20. ambivalence (*n*)
A. tension
B. inheritance
C. indecision
D. proportion

21. jocular (*adj*)
A. impassioned
B. moist
C. gymnastic
D. humorous

Exercise 11-B Sentence-Completion Quiz (30 minutes)

Please fill in the blanks, choosing the words from the list. Each word can only be used once.
请从表格所列单词中选出最符合语境的单词，填入空格，每个单词只能使用一次。

Word List

nebulous	*opulence*	*unravel*	*negligible*	*complement*
remonstrance	*vantage*	*disarray*	*insurmountable*	*unwitting*
vindictive	*ascertain*	*decipher*	*overbearing*	*resilient*
gloss over	*resurge*	*uproarious*	*interminable*	
onset	*platitude*	*intuition*	*unwieldy*	

1. But too often, willful or not, we've chosen to ________ or ignore entirely the experience of millions upon millions of others.
2. From that ________ point, he shrewdly harnessed his new influence in the struggle against the dominant establishment.
3. If we can accept others' ________, we are both virtuous and tolerant.
4. Once they had ________ that he was not a spy, they agreed to release him.
5. I'm still no closer to ________ the code.
6. I was glad of company for the last long hours of this ________ flight.
7. Such bags, though, are heavy and ________—particularly if they have to be filled far from the breach and then carried there.
8. The green wallpaper perfectly ________ the old pine of the dresser.
9. The downtown has been ________ since the commercial revitalization project was completed.
10. An amount or effect that is ________ is so small that it is not worth considering or worrying about.
11. A problem that is ________ is so great that it cannot be dealt with successfully.
12. An ________ person tries to make other people do what he or she wants in an unpleasant and forceful way.
13. Something that is ________ is strong and not easily damaged by being hit, stretched, or squeezed.
14. His personal life fell into ________ when his wife left him.

15. A __platitude__ is a statement that is considered meaningless and boring because it has been made many times before in similar situations.

16. He could __unravel__ a knot that others wouldn't even attempt.

17. He had spent several __uproarious__ evenings at the Embassy Club.

18. Whether we call it gut feelings, a "sixth sense," or something else, we have all experienced __intuition__ at one time or another.

19. The drug must be taken from the __onset__ of the infection.

20. If you describe something as __nebulous__, you mean that it is vague and not clearly defined or not easy to describe.

21. A __vindictive__ woman is desperate for revenge against the man who loved and left her.

22. __Opulence__ is the abundance of valuable resources or valuable material possessions.

23. If you describe a person or their actions as __unwitting__ you mean that the person does something or is involved in something without realizing it.

Exercise 11-C 偏难词自测练习 (30 minutes)

Please fill in the blanks, choosing the words from the list. Each word can only be used once. Then you can go back to the Word List and check your answers.
请从表格所列单词中选出与下列中文意思对应的单词，填入空格，每个单词只能使用一次。完毕之后，请回到《SAT巴朗词表：乱序版》中对应的单元，核对答案，并标注自己没有填对的单词。

Word List

unfathomable	import	poignancy	ubiquitous	conception
alimony	ensconce	cipher	subsidy	miscellany
ample	migratory	proselytize	postulate	quarantine
resumption	misdemeanor	agility	addiction	singular
problematic	replica	abstract	aquatic	deposition
inconsistency	universal	sparse	clemency	retain
perceptive	incompatible	component	reprieve	militant
prod	encroachment	abortive	pliable	quiescent
regimen	innovation	requisite	symmetry	
bulwark	credibility	malevolent	abrasive	
unkempt	microcosm	susceptible	cacophonous	
adamant	predecessor	valid	authenticate	

壁垒，防御工事；防御或保护的人 bulwark

使改变宗教或信仰 proselytize

有问题的，有疑问的 problematic

假定，基本前提 postulate

可信性 credibility

要素，成分 component

保留，留住 retain

刺，戳；激起，督促 prod

改革，革新 innovation

重要性；意思 import

充足的 ample

造成磨损的，粗糙的；生硬粗暴的 abrasive

【律】轻罪 misdemeanor

沉溺，上瘾 addiction

验证，鉴别 authenticate

杂集 miscellany

普遍的，通用的 universal

仁慈，宽厚；温和 clemency

对称，匀称 symmetry

重新开始，继续 resumption

微观世界 microcosm

好战的，好用暴力的 militant

摄生法，养生法 regimen

刺耳的；不和谐的 cacophnous

深不可测的，深奥的；无底的 unfathomable

抽象的，理论的 abstract

坚硬的；不屈不挠的 adamant

补助金，津贴 subsidy

稀少的，稀疏的 sparse

革职；宣誓作证 deposition

有洞察力的，敏锐的，有感知的 perseptive

无处不在的，普遍存在的 ubiquitous

无法共存的，不调和的 incompatible

迁移的，流浪的 migratory

有恶意的，坏心肠的 malevolent

缓刑；暂缓；暂缓处刑；给…带来缓解 reprieve

开始，构想 conception

水的 aquatic

辛酸；（感情）强烈，深刻 poignancy

失败的，夭折的 abortive

前辈，前任 predecessor

密码；无足轻重的人或物 cipher

不整洁的，（头发）蓬乱的 unkempt

敏捷，灵活 agility

前后不一致，矛盾 inconsistency

检疫，隔离 quarantine

（离婚后的）赡养费，生活费 alimony

复制品 replica

侵占，侵蚀 encroachment

必需品 requisite

安顿 ensconce

灵活的，变通的，适应性强的 pliable

易受影响的；易感动的；易感染的 susceptible

独特的，非凡的，异常的 singular

休止的，休眠的；暂时停止活动的 quiescent

有效的；有充分根据的；正当的 valid

Review: Word List 12

- □ preposterous
- □ caucus
- □ coalition
- □ legacy
- □ dispel
- □ babble
- □ placate
- □ temper
- □ brazen
- □ forsake
- □ temerity
- □ asinine
- □ monetary
- □ resolution
- □ concord
- □ entrepreneur
- □ flaunt
- □ rote
- □ antipathy
- □ superimpose
- □ fusion
- □ germinate
- □ raucous
- □ irresolute
- □ inimitable
- □ indigenous
- □ drudgery
- □ baffle
- □ elucidate
- □ intellect
- □ carnivorous
- □ pseudonym
- □ acclimate
- □ idiosyncrasy
- □ integral
- □ insatiable
- □ intimate
- □ clip
- □ facade
- □ horde
- □ tranquility
- □ diverge
- □ discourse
- □ despondent
- □ contrived
- □ misgivings
- □ intermittent
- □ appraise
- □ phobia
- □ enmity
- □ deadlock
- □ irreparable
- □ engross
- □ evasive
- □ sophisticated
- □ academic
- □ cognitive
- □ malaise
- □ explicate
- □ comprehensive
- □ cessation
- □ affable
- □ omnipresent
- □ superfluous
- □ obdurate
- □ lethargic
- □ mimicry
- □ clamor
- □ captivate
- □ embed
- □ recrimination
- □ arbitrary
- □ trajectory
- □ distinction
- □ reprisal
- □ vex
- □ pertinent
- □ authoritative
- □ edify
- □ assimilate
- □ vociferous
- □ simulate
- □ jubilation
- □ debilitate
- □ heterogeneous
- □ intricate
- □ allude
- □ annotate
- □ disconcert
- □ friction
- □ spectrum
- □ prosperity
- □ flout
- □ balk
- □ perennial
- □ colloquial
- □ depict
- □ undermine
- □ protégé
- □ misrepresent

Exercise 12

Exercise 12-A Multiple-Choice Quiz (5 minutes)

Please choose the best answer that conveys the meaning of the given word. There is only one correct choice.
请根据所给单词的意思，从A,B,C,D四个选项中找出其同义词，每题只有一个正确答案。

A 1. concord (*n*)
A. harmony
B. penchant
C. proposal
D. autonomy

C 2. raucous (*adj*)
A. elaborate
B. deciduous
C. harsh
D. ultraviolet

D 3. elucidate (*v*)
A. frost
B. deform
C. emigrate
D. explain

A 4. antipathy (*n*)
A. dislike
B. velocity
C. antecedent
D. deviation

B 5. despondent (*adj*)
A. adjacent
B. gloomy
C. prostrate
D. equatorial

C 6. edify (*v*)
A. envision
B. pledge
C. instruct
D. breed

D 7. superfluous (*adj*)
A. rear
B. ancient
C. academic
D. redundant

C 8. obdurate (*adj*)
A. alarming
B. approximate
C. stubborn
D. subsequent

B 9. pertinent (*adj*)
A. carnivorous
B. relevant
C. gradual
D. progressive

A 10. evasive (*adj*)
A. eluding
B. despotic
C. crustal
D. enormous

11. insatiable (*adj*)
A. legitimate
B. inefficient
C. regular
D. greedy

12. indigenous (*adj*)
A. indignant
B. indigent
C. native
D. natural

13. preposterous (*adj*)
A. integral
B. absurd
C. irresolute
D. arbitrary

14. captivate (*v*)
A. enclose
B. enchant
C. depict
D. misrepresent

15. flout (*v*)
A. disdain
B. explicate
C. reap
D. temper

16. lethargic (*adj*)
A. authoritative
B. heterogeneous
C. perennial
D. listless

17. brazen (*adj*)
A. dimensional
B. uplifting
C. shameless
D. inimitable

18. dispel (*v*)
A. devise
B. trace
C. scatter
D. utilize

19. forsake (*v*)
A. encompass
B. separate
C. abandon
D. divert

20. balk (*v*)
A. settle
B. check
C. indicate
D. spray

21. affable (*adj*)
A. minimal
B. horizontal
C. shrewd
D. friendly

Exercise 12-B Matching Quiz (5 minutes)

Match the words from the two columns.
从右边列表中选出和左边单词意思匹配的词汇，把它们用线连起来。

Ⓐ

assimilate	differ
intimate	show off
diverge	sprout
appraise	absorb
flaunt	feign
germinate	irritate
baffle	allude
vex	gauge
simulate	disconcert

Ⓑ

comprehensive	end
cessation	worldly-wise
mimicry	artificial
sophisticated	speech
discourse	stalemate
contrived	imitation
deadlock	inclusive

Ⓒ

omnipresent	retaliation
clamor	ubiquitous
jubilation	compromise
undermine	noise
reprisal	joy

Exercise 12-C 偏难词自测练习 (30 minutes)

Please fill in the blanks, choosing the words from the list. Each word can only be used once. Then you can go back to the Word List and check your answers.
请从表格所列单词中选出与下列中文意思对应的单词，填入空格，每个单词只能使用一次。完毕之后，请回到《SAT巴朗词表：乱序版》中对应的单元，核对答案，并标注自己没有填对的单词。

Word List

caucus
coalition
legacy
babble
placate
temper
temerity
asinine
monetary
resolution
entrepreneur
rote

superimpose
fusion
irresolute
inimitable
drudgery
intellect
carnivorous
pseudonym
acclimate
idiosyncrasy
integral
clip

façade
horde
tranquility
misgivings
intermittent
phobia
enmity
irreparable
engross
academic
cognitive
malaise

explicate
embed
recrimination
arbitrary
trajectory
distinction
authoritative
vociferous
debilitate
heterogeneous
intricate
allude

annotate
disconcert
friction
spectrum
prosperity
perennial
colloquial
depict
protégé
misrepresent

强记，死记硬背 rote
调和，调节；调音；（冶金）回火，锻炼 temper
疑虑，担忧 migivings
解释；说明；阐明 explicate
光，光谱 spectrum
鲁莽，轻率 temerity
暗指，间接提到 allude
个人癖好 idiosyncrasy
荣誉；对比，区分 distinction
联合；熔化，熔合 fusion
不能修复的，无可挽救的 irreparable
遗产，遗赠物 legacy
无决断的，犹豫不决的 irresolute
弹道；轨道 trajectory
仇恨，怨恨 enmity
无比的；无法模仿的 inimitable

武断的；任意的；霸道的 arbitrary
口语的，口头的 colloquial
评注，注释 annotate
官方的，权威的；专横的 authoritative
金钱的，货币的 monetary
幸运；繁荣，兴旺；茁壮 prosperity
剪辑，电影的片段 clip
宁静 tranquility
含糊不清地说；胡言乱语 babble
学院的；学术的，理论的 academic
整体的；构成整体所需要的 integral
大群，一帮 horde
坚定，决心 resolution
专注于 engross
把…嵌入 embed
食肉的 carnivorous
苦工，单调乏味的工作 drudgery

假名，笔名 pseudonym

多年生植物 perennial

被保护人 protégé

使适应气候，使服水土 acclimate

误传；歪曲 misrepresent

政党会议 caucus

使平静，安抚 placate

复杂的；难以理解的 intricate

愚蠢的 asinine

身体不适 malaise

（尤指大型建筑的）正面；（掩盖真实感情的）外表 facade

间歇的，断断续续的 intermittent

添加，置于他物上 superimpose

智力 intellect

认知的；认识过程的 cognitive

强烈的恐惧 phobia

企业家；立约人 entrepreneur

异类的，完全不同的；混合的 heterogenous

描述，描写 depict

使虚弱 debilitate

联合，联盟，结合 coalition

喧哗的，大声叫嚷的 vociferous

使困惑；挫败；使窘迫 disconcert

反责，反控，反唇相讥 recrimination

矛盾；摩擦 friction

Review: Word List 13

- □ bicameral
- □ effervescence
- □ hamper
- □ tribute
- □ loathe
- □ quagmire
- □ dutiful
- □ accede
- □ motif
- □ dissident
- □ centripetal
- □ wrath
- □ abdicate
- □ apocalyptic
- □ virtue
- □ allocate
- □ predilection
- □ propitiate
- □ kindred
- □ facsimile
- □ infinitesimal
- □ detrimental
- □ unmitigated
- □ practitioner
- □ guileless
- □ tenuous
- □ momentum
- □ immobility
- □ remorse
- □ harass
- □ allegiance
- □ potential
- □ ardent
- □ satire
- □ curtail
- □ virtual
- □ vigor
- □ truculence
- □ subsistence
- □ insuperable
- □ squander
- □ latent
- □ amend
- □ savor
- □ germane
- □ inopportune
- □ diversion
- □ pensive
- □ passport
- □ profligate
- □ discriminating
- □ rustic
- □ aggressor
- □ atrocity
- □ cantankerous
- □ arduous
- □ dupe
- □ allegory
- □ unrequited
- □ reciprocate
- □ equilibrium
- □ devious
- □ jollity
- □ begrudge
- □ timorous
- □ thematic
- □ discombobulated
- □ remediable
- □ climactic
- □ volition
- □ rationale
- □ retentive
- □ belabor
- □ stricture
- □ termination
- □ discrepancy
- □ promote
- □ exodus
- □ velocity
- □ strident
- □ cameo
- □ propensity
- □ vivacious
- □ reprise
- □ magnate
- □ restraint
- □ dawdle
- □ resigned
- □ timidity
- □ reiterate
- □ precocious
- □ diagnosis
- □ ponderous
- □ fiasco
- □ solemnity
- □ wary
- □ exasperate
- □ ramification
- □ amicable
- □ finale

Exercise 13

Exercise 13-A Multiple-Choice Quiz (5 minutes)

Please choose the best answer that conveys the meaning of the given word. There is only one correct choice.
请根据所给单词的意思，从A,B,C,D四个选项中找出同义词，每个题只有一个答案。

1. detrimental (*adj*)
   A. negligible
   B. harmful
   C. unwieldy
   D. dependent

2. ardent (*adj*)
   A. incentive
   B. genetic
   C. zealous
   D. resistant

3. remorse (*n*)
   A. guilt
   B. confederation
   C. canal
   D. reaction

4. discrepancy (*n*)
   A. dominance
   B. difference
   C. capillary
   D. community

5. squander (*v*)
   A. inject
   B. obtain
   C. disturb
   D. waste

6. devious (*adj*)
   A. immigrant
   B. intact
   C. dishonest
   D. particular

7. curtail (*v*)
   A. prevail
   B. restrict
   C. decay
   D. reduce

8. hamper (*v*)
   A. hinder
   B. urge
   C. hibernate
   D. migrate

9. profligate (*adj*)
   A. wasteful
   B. coercive
   C. leafy
   D. invidious

10. begrudge (*v*)
    A. expedite
    B. convey
    C. resent
    D. encroach

11. reiterate (*v*)
A. regenerate
B. repeat
C. resist
D. review

12. exasperate (*v*)
A. prey
B. log
C. plight
D. vex

13. arduous (*adj*)
A. biotic
B. strenuous
C. profound
D. crude

14. strident (*adj*)
A. climactic
B. resigned
C. harsh
D. rash

15. ponderous (*adj*)
A. vigorous
B. naturalistic
C. replete
D. clumsy

16. vivacious (*adj*)
A. animated
B. intimate
C. organic
D. muddy

17. timorous (*adj*)
A. fearful
B. remediable
C. retentive
D. microscopic

18. cantankerous (*adj*)
A. dense
B. portable
C. irritable
D. offshore

19. amend (*v*)
A. accede
B. improve
C. loathe
D. decompose

20. kindred (*adj*)
A. related
B. adverse
C. virtual
D. aggregate

Exercise 13-B Sentence-Completion Quiz (30 minutes)

Please fill in the blanks, choosing the words from the list. Each word can only be used once.
请从表格所列单词中选出最符合语境的单词，填入空格，每个单词只能使用一次。

Word List

dutiful	*unmitigated*	*reciprocate*	*satire*	*abdicate*
savor	*volition*	*tenuous*	*infinitesimal*	*wary*
solemnity	*inopportune*	*amicable*	*dupe*	*allegiance*
allocate	*discriminating*	*wrath*	*dissident*	
pensive	*propitiate*	*tribute*	*atrocity*	

1. Something that is __infinitesimal__ is extremely small.
2. You have seen duty and __allegiance__ in the determined faces of our soldiers.
3. The 1985 federal budget __allocated__ $7.3 billion for development programs.
4. He looked suddenly sombre and __pensive__.
5. Every year, memorials like this pay __tribute__ to the victims of 9/11.
6. The __atrocity__ caused widespread indignation.
7. They offered sacrifices to __propitiate__ the god.
8. The representatives of both sides __reciprocate__ formal expressions of goodwill.
9. Your __volition__ is the power you have to decide something for yourself.
10. The days of the __dutiful__ wife, who sacrifices her career for her husband, are over.
11. People did not teach their children to be __wary__ of strangers.
12. The monument was unveiled with great __solemnity__.
13. The king's unjust laws raised a great __wrath__ among the people.
14. If you describe something such as a connection, a reason, or someone's position as __tenous__, you mean that it is very uncertain or weak.
15. __Satire__ is the use of humor or exaggeration in order to show how foolish or wicked some people's behavior or ideas are.
16. The demands of the workers might often appear to them either __inopportune__ or ill-advised.
17. Someone who is __discriminating__ has the ability to recognize things that are of good quality.
18. She __savors__ her newfound freedom.
19. Gullible shoppers are easily __duped__ by unscrupulous advertisers.
20. __Dissident__ people disagree with or criticize their government or a powerful organization they belong to.
21. When people have an __amicable__ relationship, they are pleasant to each other and solve their problems without quarreling.
22. If a king or queen __abdicates__, he or she gives up being king or queen.
23. You use __unmitigated__ to emphasize that a bad situation or quality is totally bad.

Exercise 13-C 偏难词自测练习 (30 minutes)

Please fill in the blanks, choosing the words from the list. Each word can only be used once. Then you can go back to the Word List and check your answers.
请从表格所列单词中选出与下列中文意思对应的单词，填入空格，每个单词只能使用一次。完毕之后，请回到《SAT巴朗词表：乱序版》中对应的单元，核对答案，并标注自己没有填对的单词。

Word List

bicameral	guileless	diversion	rationale	restraint
effervescence	momentum	passport	retentive	dawdle
loathe	immobility	rustic	belabor	resigned
quagmire	harass	aggressor	stricture	timidity
accede	potential	allegory	termination	precocious
motif	virtual	unrequited	promote	diagnosis
centripetal	vigor	equilibrium	exodus	fiasco
apocalyptic	truculence	jollity	velocity	ramification
virtue	subsistence	thematic	cameo	finale
predilection	insuperable	discombobulated	propensity	
facsimile	latent	remediable	reprise	
practitioner	germane	climactic	magnate	

从业者，开业者 practitioner
寓言 allegory
欢腾，欢闹 jollity
沼泽，湿地；难以脱身的困境 quagmire
倾向 propensity
早熟的 precocious
乡下的；粗俗的 rustic
可挽回的 remediable
兴奋，狂喜；冒泡，起泡 effervescence

巨头，富豪，要人 magnate
促进，发扬；提拔；推广 promote
转向；消遣，娱乐 diversion
美德，德行；优点 virtue
潜在的，潜伏的 latent
护照 passport
实质的；实际上的 virtual
有保持力的；记忆力强的 retentive
结束，终止 termination

衣食，给养；存在 subsistence
平衡，均衡 equilibrium
主题，主旨 motif
坦率的，正直的 guileless
无报答的，无回报的 unrequited
不动，固定 immobility
主题的 thematic
向心的 centripetal
【音】重奏；重演；重复动作 reprise
困惑的；挫败的；打乱的，破坏的 discombobulated
启示论的，天启的 apocalyptic
不断地激怒或折磨 harass
大批离去 exodus
两院制的 bicameral
克制；限制；约束 restraint
结局，终曲 finale
惨败，大失败 fiasco
虚度，游手好闲 dawdle
精力，活力 vigor
好战；凶猛，残忍 truculence
动量；动力，冲力，势头 momentum
石雕或贝雕；特写；配角 cameo
同意 accede
侵略者，攻击者 aggressor
顶点的，高潮的 climactic
爱好，偏袒 predilection
厌恶，憎恶 loathe
摹本，精确的复制品 facsimile
羞怯，怯懦 timidity
基本原理；解释，根据，理由 rationale
顺从的，听天由命的；能容忍的 resigned
分枝，细分 ramification
喋喋不休；责骂 belabor
有潜力的 potential
有密切关系的 germane
速度，速率 velocity
约束；谴责，批评 stricture
诊断（法）；判断 diagrosis
难以克服的，不可逾越的 insuperable

Review: Word List 14

- □ paragon
- □ coagulate
- □ puny
- □ procrastinate
- □ traumatic
- □ notable
- □ posterity
- □ monotony
- □ erroneous
- □ irremediable
- □ antagonism
- □ thrifty
- □ attribute
- □ savory
- □ vigilance
- □ egotistical
- □ digression
- □ rave
- □ execute
- □ altruistic
- □ stratify
- □ acknowledge
- □ scruple
- □ paradigm
- □ diffuse
- □ imperial
- □ bogus
- □ potent
- □ endemic
- □ painstaking
- □ nutrient
- □ inception
- □ cession
- □ omnipotent
- □ cryptic
- □ flounder
- □ pragmatist
- □ rapacious
- □ acclaim
- □ tenacious
- □ glossary
- □ levity
- □ rehabilitate
- □ collusion
- □ symbiosis
- □ fickle
- □ orientation
- □ adept
- □ amoral
- □ disinclination
- □ patent
- □ forbearance
- □ benign
- □ narrative
- □ laconic
- □ acquiesce
- □ adage
- □ rejoinder
- □ audit
- □ slur
- □ confine
- □ traduce
- □ dilemma
- □ boon
- □ sect
- □ boundless
- □ multiplicity
- □ revulsion
- □ opaque
- □ prominent
- □ bask
- □ allure
- □ chastise
- □ innocuous
- □ collateral
- □ complementary
- □ stymie
- □ renounce
- □ beneficial
- □ counterpart
- □ revelry
- □ discordant
- □ euphoria
- □ verbiage
- □ condescend
- □ skeptic
- □ gauche
- □ reputable
- □ inadvertently
- □ purported
- □ debacle
- □ charlatan
- □ impassive
- □ omniscient
- □ peripheral
- □ coin
- □ anachronistic
- □ temperament
- □ profusion
- □ compensatory

Exercise 14

Exercise 14-A **Multiple-Choice Quiz (5 minutes)**

Please choose the best answer that conveys the meaning of the given word. There is only one correct choice.
请根据所给单词的意思，从A,B,C,D四个选项中找出其同义词，每题只有一个正确答案。

1. antagonism (*n*)
   A. nutrient
   B. pragmatist
   C. symbiosis
   D. hostility

2. egotistical (*adj*)
   A. notable
   B. amoral
   C. conceited
   D. boundless

3. acclaim (*v*)
   A. applaud
   B. stratify
   C. acknowledge
   D. execute

4. levity (*n*)
   A. orientation
   B. light-mindedness
   C. attribute
   D. audit

5. scruple (*v*)
   A. hesitate
   B. spear
   C. convert
   D. exaggerate

6. peripheral (*adj*)
   A. reputable
   B. beneficial
   C. narrative
   D. marginal

7. cryptic (*adj*)
   A. paramount
   B. impassive
   C. navigational
   D. mysterious

8. innocuous (*adj*)
   A. maritime
   B. overdue
   C. harmless
   D. locomotive

9. opaque (*adj*)
   A. absurd
   B. textile
   C. temporal
   D. obscure

10. discordant (*adj*)
    A. irremediable
    B. conflicting
    C. explicit
    D. abrupt

11. puny (*adj*)

A. tiny
B. cordial
C. prior
D. apparent

12. traumatic (*adj*)

A. injurious
B. flagrant
C. territorial
D. imperial

13. slur (*v*) 含糊地发音；诽谤

A. gather
B. pinpoint
C. buffer 缓冲区
D. obscure

14. allure (*v*)

A. entice
B. dazzle
C. speculate
D. recede

15. purported (*adj*)

A. polar
B. alleged
C. conscious
D. void

16. condescend (*v*)

A. sketch
B. orbit
C. deign
D. stretch

17. stymie (*v*)

A. hamper
B. submerge
C. drench
D. entice

18. chastise (*v*)

A. fertilize
B. punish
C. undergo
D. arise

19. benign (*adj*)

A. specific
B. decorative
C. amiable 友善的
D. kindly

Exercise 14-B Matching Quiz (5 minutes)

Match the words from the two columns.
从右边列表中选出和左边单词意思匹配的词汇，把它们用线连起来。

A

coagulate	*tedium*
monotony	*economical*
erroneous	*clot*
thrifty	*selfless*
vigilance	*wordy*
altruistic	*all-powerful*
diffuse	*watchfulness*
omnipotent	*incorrect*

B

flounder	*greedy*
inception	*ceding*
omniscient	*persistent*
cession	*beginning*
rapacious	*changeable*
tenacious	*complicity*
collusion	*struggle*
fickle	*all-knowing*

C

adept	*fabricate*
patent	*change*
acquiesce	*abandon*
revulsion	*assent*
renounce	*evident*
coin	*expert*

Exercise 14-C 偏难词自测练习 (30 minutes)

Please fill in the blanks, choosing the words from the list. Each word can only be used once. Then you can go back to the Word List and check your answers.
请从表格所列单词中选出与下列中文意思对应的单词，填入空格，每个单词只能使用一次。完毕之后，请回到《SAT巴朗词表：乱序版》中对应的单元，核对答案，并标注自己没有填对的单词。

Word List

paragon	paradigm	amoral	sect	skeptic
procrastinate	imperial	disinclination	boundless	gauche
notable	bogus	forbearance	multiplicity	reputable
posterity	potent	narrative	prominent	inadvertently
irremediable	endemic	laconic	bask	debacle
attribute	painstaking	adage	collateral	charlatan
savory	nutrient	rejoinder	complementary	impassive
digression	pragmatist	audit	beneficial	anachronistic
rave	glossary	confine	counterpart	temperament
execute	rehabilitate	traduce	revelry	profusion
stratify	symbiosis	dilemma	euphoria	compensatory
acknowledge	orientation	boon	verbiage	

狂喜，异常兴奋 euphoria

子孙，后裔 posterity

啰嗦，冗词 verbiage

补偿的，赔偿的 Compensatory

过分赞扬，吹捧 rave

有力的，有效的；说服力强的 potent

风味极佳的，可口的；悦人的；有益身心的 savory

延迟，耽搁 procastinate

补充的，补足的 Complementary

皇帝的；帝国的 imperial

把…分成不同的等级、阶级；使成层 stratify

担保品，抵押物 collateral

宗派，教派 sect

适应 orientation

享受乐趣；晒太阳，取暖 bask

实用主义者 pragmatist

格言，谚语 adage

诽谤，诋毁 traduce

多样性 multiplicity

使康复，恢复 rehabilitate

极丰富；挥霍；过分 profusion

（疾病）地方性的，某国家、地区或某部分人中常见的（疾病）endemic

名誉好的 reputable

典范，模范 paragon

怀疑论者 skeptic

补充物，相似物；副本 counterpart

实行；执行 execute

崩溃，灾难性的衰败 babacle

承认，认可 acknowledge

恩惠，利益 boon

不愿，厌恶 disinclination

回答；反驳 rejoinder
自制，忍耐 forbearance
不可救药的，无法改正的 irremediable
有帮助的；有用的 beneficial
禁闭；限制 confine
叙述的 narrative
（长置于书尾的）词汇表，术语表 glossary
冷漠的；冷静的；坚忍的 impassive
卓越的，显著的 prominent
非故意地；不注意地 inadvertently
离题，偏离 digression
狂欢 revelry
气质，性情 temperament
勤勉的，小心的 painstaking
值得注意的，显著的；著名的，重要的 notable
笨拙的；粗鲁的 gauche
伪造的；虚假的 bogus
属性，特征；归结于；解释 attribute
不属于道德范畴的，不道德的 amoral
模型，范例，样式 paradigm
营养物 nutrient
（进退两难的）窘境，困境 dilemma
审计 audit
【生】共生（现象）；共栖；依附关系 symbiosis
时代错误的 anachronistic
无限的，无穷的 boundless
庸医；骗子 charlatan
简洁精炼的 laconic

Review: Word List 15

- □ demystify
- □ lavish
- □ pedantic
- □ deprecate
- □ casualty
- □ overt
- □ acquire
- □ exculpate
- □ fortitude
- □ demeanor
- □ malefactor
- □ sluggish
- □ nominal
- □ disperse
- □ beneficiary
- □ malign
- □ auditory
- □ brevity
- □ decimate
- □ hoax
- □ concerted
- □ guile
- □ champion
- □ taint
- □ adjacent
- □ proximity
- □ subsequent
- □ tentative
- □ browse
- □ acrimonious
- □ assessment
- □ austere
- □ misapprehension
- □ obviate
- □ substantiate
- □ arrogance
- □ cliché
- □ wanton
- □ tender
- □ incontrovertible
- □ decry
- □ proclivity
- □ accentuate
- □ succinct
- □ audacious
- □ merger
- □ impasse
- □ tract
- □ compelling
- □ buffet
- □ celebrated
- □ defeatist
- □ noncommittal
- □ infamous
- □ countenance
- □ alienate
- □ gaffe
- □ espouse
- □ seclusion
- □ reprimand
- □ amass
- □ suppress
- □ tonic
- □ inept
- □ rapt
- □ misconception
- □ abject
- □ contagion
- □ autonomous
- □ sanguine
- □ expedite
- □ alimentary
- □ vehement
- □ marsupial
- □ repudiate
- □ diabolical
- □ intangible
- □ insolence
- □ chauvinist
- □ rebuke
- □ rig
- □ ambidextrous
- □ paramount
- □ depreciate
- □ illicit
- □ vaporize
- □ accord
- □ imputation
- □ gullible
- □ impudence
- □ pernicious
- □ corroborate
- □ mammoth
- □ felon
- □ temperate
- □ calamity
- □ objective
- □ wry
- □ adhere
- □ enfranchise

Exercise 15

Exercise 15-A Multiple-Choice Quiz (5 minutes)

Please choose the best answer that conveys the meaning of the given word. There is only one correct choice.
请根据所给单词的意思，从A,B,C,D四个选项中找出其同义词，每题只有一个正确答案。

1. audacious (*adj*)
   A. adjacent
   B. infamous
   C. bold
   D. celebrated

2. austere (*adj*)
   A. compelling
   B. objective
   C. stern
   D. auditory

3. impudence (*n*)
   A. insolence
   B. despotism
   C. accord
   D. degradation

4. cliché (*n*)
   A. brevity
   B. arrogance
   C. beneficiary
   D. platitude

5. exculpate (*v*)
   A. acquire
   B. absolve
   C. browse
   D. intermeddle

6. lavish (*adj*)
   A. atomic
   B. static
   C. luxurious
   D. comparative

7. malign (*v*)
   A. defame
   B. suppress
   C. incline
   D. agitate

8. reprimand (*v*)
   A. expedite
   B. infringe
   C. vaporize
   D. rebuke

9. corroborate (*v*)
   A. adhere
   B. languish
   C. substantiate
   D. mist

10. deprecate (*v*)
    A. condense
    B. decry
    C. usurp
    D. entangle

11. tender (*v*)
A. project
B. secure
C. demonstrate
D. extend

12. champion (*v*)
A. espouse
B. cement
C. retrieve
D. breed

13. tonic (*adj*)
A. additional
B. void
C. invigorating
D. conscious

14. autonomous (*adj*)
A. mid-continental
B. incontrovertible
C. self-governing
D. coastal

15. overt (*adj*)
A. tropic
B. oval
C. short-lived
D. manifest

16. succinct (*adj*)
A. exterior
B. brief
C. prevalent
D. lamentable

17. seclusion (*n*)
A. merger
B. trace
C. alliance
D. solitude

18. repudiate (*v*)
A. reject
B. forfeit
C. adorn
D. recede

19. misapprehension (*n*)
A. malefactor
B. misconception
C. credibility
D. proximity

20. accentuate (*v*)
A. overstate
B. undergo
C. emphasize
D. intervene

Exercise 15-B Sentence-Completion Quiz (30 minutes)

Please fill in the blanks, choosing the words from the list. Each word can only be used once.
请从表格所列单词中选出最符合语境的单词，填入空格，每个单词只能使用一次。

Word List

casualty	disperse	alienate	demeanor	contagion
decimate	illicit	vehement	countenance	sanguine
obviate	nominal	inept	taint	proclivity
noncommittal	sluggish	hoax	paramount	alimentary
depreciate	tentative	impasse	concerted	abject

1. He had the disease of ______ canal.
2. The party's opposition was a major driver of the fiscal ______ that halted federal operations and risked a debt default.
3. Gender equality is ______ for a better society.
4. This kind of moth is responsible for ______ thousands of trees in our town.
5. A parachute can be used to ______ disaster.
6. We'd better not ______ ourselves from the colleagues.
7. He seemed quite ______ about his chances of success.
8. He is under investigation for receiving ______ funds.
9. You use ______ to indicate that someone or something is supposed to have a particular identity or status, but in reality does not have it.
10. A more ______ economy will make it harder for the government to achieve its fiscal targets.
11. They don't really think of the real meaning of ______ as working together.
12. I asked him if he approved of our plan, but he was ______.
13. ______ is the spreading of a particular disease by someone touching another person who is already affected by the disease.
14. This policy has turned out to be an ______ failure.
15. She suddenly became very ______ and agitated, jumping around and shouting.
16. Parents fret that staring at screens all day has made youngsters socially ______ face-to-face.
17. A ______ is a trick in which someone tells people a lie.
18. Mr. Jones was the first ______ of the firm's cut-backs.
19. ______ agreements, plans, or arrangements are not definite or certain, but have been made as a first step.
20. If someone will not ______ something, they do not agree with it and will not allow it to happen.

21. A proclivity is a tendency to behave in a particular way or to like a particular thing, often a bad way or thing.

22. Pornography decimates taints the young mind.

23. Your demeanor is the way you behave, which gives people an impression of your character and feelings.

24. If something such as a currency depreciates it loses some of its original value.

25. Riot police with tear gas dispersed some parts of the crowd.

Exercise 15-C 偏难词自测练习 (30 minutes)

Please fill in the blanks, choosing the words from the list. Each word can only be used once. Then you can go back to the Word List and check your answers.

请从表格所列单词中选出与下列中文意思对应的单词，填入空格，每个单词只能使用一次。完毕之后，请回到《SAT巴朗词表：乱序版》中对应的单元，核对答案，并标注自己没有填对的单词。

Word List

demystify	*subsequent*	*compelling*	*expedite*	*imputation*
pedantic	*browse*	*buffet*	*marsupial*	*gullible*
acquire	*acrimonious*	*celebrated*	*diabolical*	*pernicious*
fortitude	*assessment*	*defeatist*	*intangible*	*mammoth*
malefactor	*substantiate*	*infamous*	*insolence*	*felon*
beneficiary	*arrogance*	*gaffe*	*chauvinist*	*temperate*
auditory	*wanton*	*espouse*	*rebuke*	*calamity*
brevity	*incontrovertible*	*amass*	*rig*	*objective*
guile	*decry*	*suppress*	*ambidextrous*	*wry*
adjacent	*merger*	*rapt*	*vaporize*	*adhere*
proximity	*tract*	*misconception*	*accord*	*enfranchise*

证明，证实；支持 substantiate　　　　地方，地域；小册子 tract

傲慢无礼 insolence　　　　评估，评价 assessment

误解，错觉 misconception

（企业等的）吞并；结合 merger

获得 acquire

盲目的爱国者 chauvinist

犯罪分子 malefactor

吃草；浏览 browse

失败主义的；失败主义者 defeatist

后来的，随后的 subsequent

易受骗的 gullible

狡诈；诡计 guile

黏附 adhere

著名的 celebrated

（关于）听觉的 auditory

装配；操纵 rig

归咎；非难；责备 imputation

拥护，支持 espouse

巨大的；体积庞大的 mammoth

傲慢 arrogance

感觉不到的，无形的 intangible

使非神秘化，澄清 demystify

恶魔似的，残忍的 diabolical

无可辩驳的，不容置疑的 incontrovertible

失礼，失态 gaffe

有袋动物 marsupial

接近，亲近 proximity

坚韧，刚毅；勇气 fortitude

两手都善用的 ambidextrous

饮食柜台；自助餐 buffet

客观的，无偏见的；目标，目的 objective

指责，谴责 rebuke

简洁 brevity

有节制的，适度的；（气候等）温和的 temperate

使蒸发，使汽化 vaporize

被深深吸引的，入迷的 rapt

无节制的；肆意的；不贞洁的 wanton

收集，积聚 amass

强烈反对，谴责；贬低，轻视 decry

给予…公民权（尤指选举权） enfranchise

促进，加快（进程） expedite

抑制，克服，约束 suppress

迂腐的，学究式的 pedantic

有害的，恶性的 pernicious

强制的；有说服力的 compelling

臭名昭著的 infamous

（言辞、态度等）尖刻的 acrimonious

一致，符合 accord

受益人 beneficiary

扭曲的；嘲弄的 wry

（法律）重罪犯 felon

临近的，接近的 adjacent

灾难，不幸 calamity

Review: Word List 16

- □ warranty
- □ entity
- □ saturate
- □ repulsion
- □ amorous
- □ inalienable
- □ passive
- □ germinal
- □ ceremonious
- □ prodigal
- □ ameliorate
- □ venerate
- □ hypercritical
- □ genesis
- □ didactic
- □ supposition
- □ incentive
- □ baroque
- □ parasite
- □ ascendancy
- □ absolute
- □ vestige
- □ neologism
- □ verve
- □ deplore
- □ optimum
- □ garbled
- □ vicarious
- □ arid
- □ ephemeral
- □ sustain
- □ flag
- □ hardy
- □ plummet
- □ exertion
- □ corrosive
- □ inarticulate
- □ indubitable
- □ elated
- □ wither
- □ lampoon
- □ abundant
- □ imprudent
- □ incidence
- □ plutocracy
- □ tenure
- □ chivalrous
- □ confound
- □ decadence
- □ heed
- □ commodious
- □ inveterate
- □ disparity
- □ rationalize
- □ braggart
- □ bluff
- □ disgruntle
- □ context
- □ prophetic
- □ exceptionable
- □ substantive
- □ perturb
- □ misconstrue
- □ disenfranchise
- □ exegesis
- □ conformity
- □ sage
- □ defiance
- □ finesse
- □ extrinsic
- □ tyranny
- □ deterrent
- □ couple
- □ secular
- □ amity
- □ lurid
- □ iota
- □ distant
- □ profound
- □ levy
- □ atheistic
- □ excerpt
- □ martyr
- □ bolt
- □ ingenious
- □ auspicious
- □ quandary
- □ innovative
- □ apathy
- □ salubrious
- □ specious
- □ buoyant
- □ irrelevant
- □ incapacitate
- □ random
- □ forestall
- □ latitude
- □ revert
- □ indefatigable
- □ linger

Exercise 16

Exercise 16-A Multiple-Choice Quiz (5 minutes)

Please choose the best answer that conveys the meaning of the given word. There is only one correct choice.
请根据所给单词的意思，从A,B,C,D四个选项中找出其同义词，每题只有一个正确答案。

1. warranty (*n*)
A. entity
B. supposition
C. trace
D. guarantee

2. prodigal (*adj*)
A. wasteful
B. absolute
C. arid
D. corrosive

3. repulsion (*n*)
A. apprehension
B. tenure
C. clash
D. distaste

4. venerate (*v*)
A. revere
B. vanish
C. vindicate
D. revive

5. germinal (*adj*)
A. passive
B. benevolent
C. creative
D. ceremonious

6. deplore (*v*)
A. regret
B. couple
C. excerpt
D. deject

7. elated (*adj*)
A. distant
B. profound
C. innovative
D. overjoyed

8. secular (*adj*)
A. random
B. worldly
C. ingenious
D. irrelevant

9. ephemeral (*adj*)
A. permanent
B. hardy
C. fleeting
D. abundant

10. lurid (*adj*)
A. atheistic
B. artificial
C. precise
D. sensational

11. indefatigable (*adj*)
A. substantive
B. extrinsic
C. tireless
D. inalienable

12. wither (*v*)
A. withdraw
B. gather
C. wilt
D. pertain

13. confound (*v*)
A. puzzle
B. compound
C. overcast
D. rotate

14. plummet (*v*)
A. fall
B. exert
C. wrap
D. abuse

15. deterrent (*n*)
A. deterioration
B. grievance
C. terrorism
D. hindrance

16. quandary (*n*)
A. imagination
B. dilemma
C. inveteracy
D. disposition

17. incentive (*v*)
A. motive
B. context
C. conformity
D. indication

18. ascendancy (*n*)
A. domination
B. aspiration
C. donation
D. appearance

19. disparity (*n*)
A. commence
B. acquaintance
C. difference
D. tyranny

Exercise 16-B Matching Quiz (5 minutes)

Match the words from the two columns.
从右边列表中选出和左边单词意思匹配的词汇，把它们用线连起来。

Ⓐ

amorous	*speechless*
hypercritical	*loving*
genesis	*origin*
didactic	*droop*
parasite	*overcritical*
optimum	*best*
flag	*freeloader*
inarticulate	*teaching*

Ⓑ

indubitable	*dissatisfy*
imprudent	*disturb*
heed	*deep-rooted*
inveterate	*injudicious*
disgruntle	*consider*
prophetic	*unquestionable*
exceptionable	*foreshadowing*
perturb	*objectionable*

Ⓒ

misconstrue	*impose*
disenfranchise	*resistance*
defiance	*cheerful*
amity	*friendship*
levy	*dawdle*
buoyant	*misjudge*
linger	*deprive*

Exercise 16-C 偏难词自测练习 (30 minutes)

Please fill in the blanks, choosing the words from the list. Each word can only be used once. Then you can go back to the Word List and check your answers.
请从表格所列单词中选出与下列中文意思对应的单词，填入空格，每个单词只能使用一次。完毕之后，请回到《SAT巴朗词表：乱序版》中对应的单元，核对答案，并标注自己没有填对的单词。

Word List

entity	garbled	chivalrous	extrinsic	innovative
saturate	vicarious	decadence	tyranny	apathy
inalienable	arid	commodious	couple	salubrious
passive	sustain	rationalize	iota	specious
ceremonious	hardy	braggart	distant	irrelevant
ameliorate	exertion	bluff	profound	incapacitate
supposition	corrosive	context	atheistic	random
baroque	lampoon	substantive	excerpt	forestall
absolute	abundant	exegesis	martyr	latitude
vestige	incidence	conformity	bolt	revert
neologism	plutocracy	sage	ingenious	
verve	tenure	finesse	auspicious	

消极的，被动的 passive

极少量 iota

承受；支撑，维持 sustain

颓废，衰退 decadence

痕迹，残余 vestige

圣人 sage

不相干的，不切题的 irrelevant

混淆的，歪曲的 garbled

发生频率；发生，出现 incidence

实体的，真正的；本质的；坚固的 substantive

实体 entity

精密的技巧 finesse

上下文 context

财阀政府 plutocracy

吉兆的，幸运的 auspicious

直率的，坦率的 bluff

专制，暴政 tyranny

任意的，随便的 random

假定，推测 supposition

吹牛的人 braggart

（用文章）挖苦，讥讽；讽刺文章 lampoon

符合，一致 conformity

似是而非的；华而不实的 specious

替代别人的，替代的 vicarious

丰富的，充裕的 abundant

先发制人，预防 forestall

浸透，使充满 saturate

没有兴趣，冷漠 apathy

彬彬有礼的；侠义的；勇武的 chivalrous

气魄，神韵；活力 verve

文过饰非，自圆其说 rationalize

努力；费力 exertion

外在的；非固有的；非本质的 extrinsic

使…无力量或能力 incapacitate

改善，改进 ameliorate

回复；恢复 revert

机灵的，足智多谋的 ingenians

（土地、职位等的）保有任期 tenure

殉道者，烈士；受难者 martyr

新词 neologism

结合 couple

不可剥夺的；（指权利等）不能让与的

inalienable

有益健康的 salubrious

革新的，创新的 innovative

正式的，隆重的 ceremonious

干旱的；贫瘠的 arid

宽敞舒适的 commodious

强壮的；坚强的；吃苦耐劳的 hardy

冷淡的，疏远的 distant

深的；深奥的；完全的 profound

（尤指对圣经内容的）详细解释，诠释

exegesis

完全的，无限制的，绝对的 absolute

选择余地，自由度 latitude

无神论的 atheistic

腐蚀的 corrosive

（诗、书或音乐的）摘抄，目录；摘录，引用 exerpt

门闩；螺栓；一匹（布） bolt

巴洛克风格的 baroque

Review: Word List 17

- □ neutral
- □ fester
- □ propriety
- □ phenomena
- □ polarize
- □ unobtrusive
- □ ostentatious
- □ deride
- □ juncture
- □ venerable
- □ consensus
- □ application
- □ boisterous
- □ remiss
- □ tacit
- □ parity
- □ tautology
- □ equivocate
- □ stamina
- □ assurance
- □ implicit
- □ rousing
- □ foresight
- □ desolate
- □ explicit
- □ provocative
- □ prudent
- □ document
- □ dichotomy
- □ pacifist
- □ breach
- □ marshal
- □ beseech
- □ stigma
- □ concise
- □ predator
- □ lofty
- □ impediment
- □ converge
- □ docile
- □ initiate
- □ rhetorical
- □ pretentious
- □ ruminate
- □ denouement
- □ communal
- □ inundate
- □ tensile
- □ satirical
- □ caricature
- □ tantalize
- □ galvanize
- □ buttress
- □ gamut
- □ edict
- □ trigger
- □ dwarf
- □ woe
- □ judicious
- □ falter
- □ milieu
- □ emancipate
- □ reticence
- □ ratify
- □ breadth
- □ subside
- □ callous
- □ repress
- □ plight
- □ stereotype
- □ alliteration
- □ sinister
- □ mushroom
- □ artifice
- □ condemn
- □ veracity
- □ cite
- □ trepidation
- □ evanescent
- □ avenge
- □ schism
- □ recapitulate
- □ supersede
- □ avarice
- □ collaborate
- □ nomenclature
- □ banal
- □ oblique
- □ pessimism
- □ refrain
- □ endorse
- □ blasphemy
- □ renegade
- □ opportunist
- □ atone
- □ bureaucracy
- □ attentive
- □ agitate
- □ mercurial
- □ subversive

Exercise 17

Exercise 17-A Multiple-Choice Quiz (5 minutes)

Please choose the best answer that conveys the meaning of the given word. There is only one correct choice.
请根据所给单词的意思，从A,B,C,D四个选项中找出其同义词，每题只有一个正确答案。

D 1. venerable (*adj*)
A. vulnerable
B. rhetorical
C. communal
D. honorable

B 2. remiss (*adj*)
A. tensile
B. negligent
C. attentive
D. generic

C 3. galvanize (*v*)
A. overshadow
B. desert
C. stimulate
D. adduce

B 4. satirical (*adj*)
A. capable
B. mocking
C. reproductive
D. vigorous

A 5. inundate (*v*)
A. flood
B. agitate
C. engrave
D. fracture

C 6. condemn (*v*)
A. dissipate
B. metabolize
C. censure
D. mismatch

D 7. mercurial (*adj*)
A. merciful
B. complementary
C. haughty
D. capricious

B 8. beseech (*v*)
A. cite
B. beg
C. document
D. fortify

A 9. buttress (*v*)
A. endorse
B. recharge
C. predominate
D. tap

A 10. deride (*v*)
A. ridicule
B. trigger
C. initiate
D. dwarf

11. converge (*v*)
A. nestle
B. meet
C. collaborate
D. furnish

12. consensus (*n*)
A. foresight
B. dictatorship
C. agreement
D. pacifist

13. ostentatious (*adj*)
A. infant
B. prudent
C. pretentious
D. implicit

14. plight (*n*)
A. augmentation
B. surplus
C. stereotype
D. dilemma

15. veracity (*n*)
A. solidarity
B. shuttle
C. honesty
D. escalation

16. propriety (*n*)
A. fitness
B. phenomena
C. cultivation
D. assurance

17. application (*n*)
A. attention
B. predator
C. opulence
D. breadth

18. unobtrusive (*adj*)
A. neutral
B. inconspicuous
C. explicit
D. rousing

19. reticence (*v*)
A. reserve
B. succor
C. artifice
D. parity

Exercise 17-B Sentence-Completion Quiz (30 minutes)

Please fill in the blanks, choosing the words from the list. Each word can only be used once.
请从表格所列单词中选出最符合语境的单词，填入空格，每个单词只能使用一次。

Word List

woe	supersede	tacit	edict	boisterous
ratify	stigma	emancipate	ruminate	callous
juncture	marshal	mushroom	banal	provocative
impediment	atone	judicious	repress	sinister
docile	falter	desolate	subside	

1. His ______ words only fueled the argument further.
2. Someone who has a speech ______ has a disability that makes speaking difficult.
3. A person or animal that is ______ is quiet, not aggressive, and easily controlled.
4. Labor-saving devices have ______ women from kitchen drudgery.
5. Her hobby ______ into a thriving business.
6. He wished to ______ for the wrong he had done.
7. The wind ______ to a calm.
8. The government issued an ______ banning public demonstrations.
9. ______ is a condition of deep suffering from misfortune, affliction, or grief.
10. The house was ______, ready to be torn down.
11. The foreign visitors were ______ into the presence of the king.
12. At a particular ______ means at a particular point in time, especially when it is a very important time in a process or series of events.
13. If something has a ______ attached to it, people think it is something to be ashamed of.
14. ______ planning now can prevent problems later.
15. As people grow older, they begin to ______ on the uncertainty of life.
16. Something that is ______ seems evil or harmful.
17. The business ______ due to poor management.
18. Your silence may be taken to mean ______ agreement.
19. When national leaders or organizations ______ a treaty or written agreement, they make it official by giving their formal approval to it, usually by signing it or voting for it.
20. If you describe something as ______, you do not like it because you think it is so ordinary that it is not at all effective or interesting.
21. A selfish and ______ young man never shows sympathy for others.
22. The use of robots will someday ______ manual labor.
23. The fans at the baseball game became particularly ______ after the home run.
24. The army quickly ______ the rebellion in the provincial city and restored order.

Exercise 17-C 偏难词自测练习 (30 minutes)

Please fill in the blanks, choosing the words from the list. Each word can only be used once. Then you can go back to the Word List and check your answers.
请从表格所列单词中选出与下列中文意思对应的单词，填入空格，每个单词只能使用一次。完毕之后，请回到《SAT巴朗词表：乱序版》中对应的单元，核对答案，并标注自己没有填对的单词。

Word List

neutral	explicit	denouement	artifice	refrain
fester	prudent	communal	cite	endorse
phenomena	document	tensile	trepidation	blasphemy
polarize	dichotomy	caricature	evanescent	renegade
parity	pacifist	tantalize	avenge	opportunist
tautology	breach	gamut	schism	bureaucracy
equivocate	concise	trigger	recapitulate	attentive
stamina	predator	dwarf	avarice	agitate
assurance	lofty	milieu	collaborate	subversive
implicit	initiate	breadth	nomenclature	
rousing	rhetorical	stereotype	oblique	
foresight	pretentious	alliteration	pessimism	

开始，发起；接纳…为会员 initiate
环境；表达方式 milieu
溃烂，发炎；激怒 fester
短暂的，瞬间的 evanescent
使显得矮小 dwarf
和平主义者 pacifist
现象 phenomena
自命不凡的，自夸的 pretentious
引发，引起 trigger
热烈的，鼓舞人的，活跃的 rousing
节制，避免；制止 refrain
含糊其辞，支吾其词 equivocate
术语；命名法 nomenclature
煽动，使不安 agitate
头韵 alliteration
亵渎，渎神 blasphemy
概况，总结 recapitulate
技巧，诡计 artifice

相同，同等 parity

漫画，夸张的描述；歪曲 caricature

为…提供文件（或证据等） document

逗弄，使备尝渴望而不可及之苦 tantalize

谨慎的 prudent

赞同，支持 endorse

高耸的；崇高的 lofty

宽度，幅度 breadth

整个范围 gamut

毅力，持久力 stamina

报仇 avenge

食肉动物，捕食者；掠夺者 predator

机会主义者 opportunist

使两极化 polarize

合作，协作 collaborate

注意的，留心的；体贴的 attentive

清楚的；明确的；直言的 explicit

背叛者，变节者；背叛的，谋叛的 renegade

悲观主义，悲观 pessimism

官僚主义，官僚机构 bureaucracy

含蓄的，暗示的 implicit

修辞学的；华丽的，浮夸的 rhetorical

对分；分叉 dichotomy

可拉长的，可伸长的 tensile

保证；确信；自信 assurance

公共的；社区的 communal

违背，违反；裂缝 breach

中立的，不偏不倚的 neutral

结局；戏剧的最后结果 denouement

简明的，简洁的 concise

陈词滥调；老套；固定的形象 stereotype

分裂，不和 schism

恐惧，惶恐 trepidation

远见性，深谋远虑 foresight

间接的；倾斜的 oblique

引用；传唤 cite

同义反复，重复 tautology

颠覆性的，破坏性的 subversive

贪婪 avarice

Review: Word List 18

- □ acute
- □ prologue
- □ belie
- □ reprove
- □ grate
- □ inclusive
- □ delve
- □ mercenary
- □ monumental
- □ rigid
- □ host
- □ turbulence
- □ artisan
- □ garner
- □ prognosis
- □ antecede
- □ scanty
- □ annihilate
- □ mutability
- □ dissertation
- □ protract
- □ ramify
- □ nicety
- □ cognizance
- □ dynamic
- □ reconcile
- □ pedestrian
- □ contingent
- □ amputate
- □ intrude
- □ connoisseur
- □ tedious
- □ recast
- □ secession
- □ compliant
- □ generic
- □ adjunct
- □ trivial
- □ boorish
- □ exult
- □ urbane
- □ censorious
- □ brusque
- □ anecdote
- □ prevaricate
- □ orator
- □ ensemble
- □ definitive
- □ disconsolate
- □ upbraid
- □ reminiscence
- □ castigate
- □ cumulative
- □ shrewd
- □ hazardous
- □ sporadic
- □ arrest
- □ extrovert
- □ dexterous
- □ analogous
- □ ruthless
- □ graduated
- □ insightful
- □ grotesque
- □ exhilarating
- □ subterfuge
- □ humility
- □ migrant
- □ fallible
- □ cede
- □ emend
- □ bustle
- □ faculty
- □ distort
- □ exhaustive
- □ dismay
- □ hostility
- □ studied
- □ wane
- □ versatile
- □ novice
- □ apocryphal
- □ catastrophe
- □ deference
- □ diligence
- □ engage
- □ knotty
- □ collate
- □ neophyte
- □ beeline
- □ burgeon
- □ anthropoid
- □ altercation
- □ commemorate
- □ blare
- □ perspicacious
- □ usurp
- □ inherent
- □ intransigence
- □ prevail

Exercise 18

Exercise 18-A Multiple-Choice Quiz (5 minutes)

Please choose the best answer that conveys the meaning of the given word. There is only one correct choice.
请根据所给单词的意思，从A,B,C,D四个选项中找出其同义词，每题只有一个正确答案。

1. mutability (*n*)
   A. nicety
   B. host
   C. fickleness
   D. artisan

2. belie (*v*)
   A. contradict
   B. grate
   C. ramify
   D. intrude

3. secession (*n*)
   A. access
   B. restraint
   C. abridgment
   D. withdrawal

4. studied (*adj*)
   A. versatile
   B. deliberate
   C. insightful
   D. downright

5. cede (*v*)
   A. engage
   B. burgeon
   C. dismay
   D. yield

6. perspicacious (*adj*)
   A. graduated
   B. cumulative
   C. shrewd
   D. definitive

7. disconsolate (*adj*)
   A. generic
   B. sad
   C. jealous
   D. dynamic

8. compliant (*adj*)
   A. inherent
   B. intentional
   C. perceptual
   D. obedient

9. exhilarating (*adj*)
   A. credible
   B. audio
   C. cheering
   D. nutritional

10. hazardous (*adj*)
   A. inaccurate
   B. paradoxical
   C. dangerous
   D. ancestral

11. dexterous (*adj*)

A. skillful
B. cellular
C. constant
D. fatty

12. amputate (*v*)

A. prune
B. render
C. sponge
D. evoke

13. reconcile (*v*)

A. format
B. harmonize
C. domesticate
D. soften

14. annihilate (*v*)

A. despise
B. proportionate
C. insulate
D. devastate

15. novice (*n*)

A. diligence
B. blare
C. humidity
D. apprentice

16. usurp (*v*)

A. arrest
B. arrange
C. seize
D. coil

17. pedestrian (*adj*)

A. imaginative
B. variable
C. tedious
D. awesome

Exercise 18-B Matching Quiz (5 minutes)

Match the words from the two columns.
从右边列表中选出和左边单词意思匹配的词汇，把它们用线连起来。

A

delve	precede
monumental	conditional
antecede	rejoice
dissertation	story
protract	massive
contingent	essay
anecdote	prolong
exult	dig

B

prologue	trickery
analogous	comprehensive
ruthless	introduction
subterfuge	comparable
exhaustive	cruel

C

catastrophe	calamity
knotty	trifling
collate	compare
commemorate	abrupt
sporadic	intricate
brusque	forecast
trivial	celebrate
prognosis	occasional

Exercise 18-C 偏难词自测练习 (30 minutes)

Please fill in the blanks, choosing the words from the list. Each word can only be used once. Then you can go back to the Word List and check your answers.
请从表格所列单词中选出与下列中文意思对应的单词，填入空格，每个单词只能使用一次。完毕之后，请回到《SAT巴朗词表：乱序版》中对应的单元，核对答案，并标注自己没有填对的单词。

Word List

acute	cognizance	ensemble	migrant	engage
reprove	dynamic	definitive	fallible	neophyte
grate	intrude	upbraid	emend	beeline
inclusive	connoisseur	reminiscence	bustle	burgeon
mercenary	tedious	castigate	faculty	anthropoid
rigid	recast	cumulative	distort	altercation
host	generic	shrewd	dismay	blare
turbulence	adjunct	arrest	hostility	inherent
artisan	boorish	extrovert	wane	intransigence
garner	urbane	graduated	versatile	prevail
scanty	censorious	insightful	apocryphal	
ramify	prevaricate	grotesque	deference	
nicety	orator	humility	diligence	

撒谎；支吾，搪塞 prevaricate
多才多艺的，多面手的 versatile
决定性的，最后的 definitive
大量；主人，东道主；宿主 host
改写；重塑，重置 recast
激烈的争论，争吵 altercation
彬彬有礼的，文雅的；都市化的 urbane
发出刺耳的声音；使气恼；磨损 grate
累积的 cumulative
粗鲁的；不敏感的 boorish
缺乏的，不足的 scanty
敏锐的；急性的，剧烈的 acute
性格外向的人 extrovert
勤勉，勤奋 diligence
停止；吸引注意 arrest
唯利是图的 mercenary
易犯错误的 fallible
才能；（大学）全体教师 faculty
奇怪的，怪诞的 grotesque
直线 beeline
奔忙；充满 bustle
坚决的；严格的；坚硬的 rigid
责备，叱责 upbraid
单调乏味的；冗长的；沉闷的 tedious
变小；衰退，结束；月亏 wane
回忆，怀旧 reminiscence
获得，收集，储藏 garner
敌意，敌视 hostility

伪的，杜撰的 apocryphal
骚乱，动荡 turbulence
使失望；使惊慌 dismay
附件，辅助物 adjunct
迁移的，移居的 migrant
认识 cognizance
与人类相似的 anthropoid
谦逊，谦恭 humility
固有的，与生俱来的 inherent
新信徒；初学者，敌手 neophyte
有活力的，生机勃勃的 dynamic
迅速成长；萌芽 burgeon
有洞察力的，有深刻见解的 insightful
不妥协，不让步 intransigence
鉴赏家 connoisseur
工匠，技工 artisan
遵从，敬重 deference
挑剔的，吹毛求疵的 censorious
训斥，谴责 reprove
严厉批评；惩罚 castigate
闯入，侵入 intrude
演说家 orator
一般的，普通的 generic
小乐队，合奏组；成套的东西；套服 ensemble
微妙之处；精确；细节，细微之处；美好 nicety
机灵的，精明的 shrewd
（使）分枝，（使）分叉 ramify
包括的，包罗广泛的 inclusive

扭歪，使变形 distort

分等级的，分阶段的 graduated

劝诱；战胜，获胜 prevail

响而刺耳的声音；耀眼的光 blare

使参与；吸引；雇用；保证；交战 engage

校订，修改 emend

Review: Word List 19

- □ travail
- □ machination
- □ subjective
- □ blatant
- □ muster
- □ probe
- □ avid
- □ disparage
- □ avert
- □ subtlety
- □ mishap
- □ irreconcilable
- □ converse
- □ insubstantial
- □ pretext
- □ immaculate
- □ unerringly
- □ insurrection
- □ obligatory
- □ biased
- □ conducive
- □ privation
- □ enunciate
- □ dissonance
- □ regime
- □ facile
- □ encompass
- □ prosaic
- □ duration
- □ compile
- □ bent
- □ resolve
- □ fanaticism
- □ volatile
- □ sham
- □ articulate
- □ coup
- □ laborious
- □ witless
- □ tenacity
- □ whet
- □ equinox
- □ impetuous
- □ clench
- □ contentious
- □ corporeal
- □ quixotic
- □ exacting
- □ allege
- □ mentor
- □ grandeur
- □ seasoned
- □ advocate
- □ disclose
- □ discrete
- □ swerve
- □ pithy
- □ headstrong
- □ impair
- □ gravity
- □ conclusive
- □ enhance
- □ disseminate
- □ concur
- □ devoid
- □ axiom
- □ furor
- □ cohesion
- □ impartial
- □ bohemian
- □ inscrutable
- □ serenity
- □ porous
- □ induce
- □ raze
- □ effectual
- □ chimerical
- □ proxy
- □ indignation
- □ capacity
- □ extenuate
- □ concentric
- □ abduction
- □ sarcasm
- □ rectitude
- □ chagrin
- □ propagate
- □ invalidate
- □ homage
- □ concoct
- □ clout
- □ impassable
- □ congenial
- □ flux
- □ conceit
- □ goad
- □ ignominy
- □ heyday
- □ covert
- □ provisional
- □ scrutinize

Exercise 19

Exercise 19-A Multiple-Choice Quiz (5 minutes)

Please choose the best answer that conveys the meaning of the given word. There is only one correct choice.
请根据所给单词的意思，从A,B,C,D四个选项中找出其同义词，每题只有一个正确答案。

1. prosaic (*adj*)
A. dull
B. irksome
C. irreconcilable
D. biased

2. volatile (*adj*)
A. insubstantial
B. subjective
C. changeable
D. witless

3. privation (*n*)
A. converse
B. subtlety
C. exertion
D. hardship

4. pretext (*n*)
A. duration
B. excuse
C. vanity
D. mentor

5. disseminate (*v*)
A. enhance
B. scatter
C. concur
D. induce

6. contentious (*adj*)
A. exacting
B. agreeable
C. headstrong
D. quarrelsome

7. impetuous (*adj*)
A. violent
B. conclusive
C. articulate
D. obligatory

8. machination (*n*)
A. regime
B. plot
C. gravity
D. cohesion

9. serenity (*n*)
A. proxy
B. capacity
C. calmness
D. axiom

10. discrete (*adj*)
A. aristocratic
B. discreet
C. odd
D. separate

11. grandeur (*n*)
A. gullibility
B. splendor
C. flux
D. heyday

12. bent (*n*)
A. inclination
B. kinship
C. ecstasy
D. timber

13. dissonance (*n*)
A. discord
B. discard
C. disparity
D. dissatisfaction

14. avid (*adj*)
A. intrinsic
B. greedy
C. monetary
D. insecure

15. insurrection (*n*)
A. cement
B. proton
C. recurrence
D. rebellion

16. fanaticism (*n*)
A. nucleus
B. proposal
C. foresight
D. zeal

17. travail (*n*)
A. integrity
B. agony
C. sarcasm
D. residual

18. conducive (*adj*)
A. circumstantial
B. molecular
C. navigable
D. instrumental

19. blatant (*adj*)
A. flagrant
B. irresistible
C. amphibian
D. pendulous

Exercise 19-B Sentence-Completion Quiz (30 minutes)

Please fill in the blanks, choosing the words from the list. Each word can only be used once.
请从表格所列单词中选出最符合语境的单词，填入空格，每个单词只能使用一次。

Word List

congenial	homage	muster	invalidate	probe
clout	disparage	chagrin	laborious	devoid
avert	conceit	tenacity	Indignation	covert
abduction	inscrutable	seasoned	ignominy	scrutinize

1. A ___seasoned___ traveller is a person who has travelled a lot.
2. ___Homage___ is respect shown toward someone or something you admire, or to a person in authority.
3. If you ___disparage___ someone or something, you speak about them in a way which shows that you do not have a good opinion of them.
4. The country has become ___inscrutable___, remote and incomprehensible even for governments.
5. He travelled around West Africa trying to ___muster___ support for his movement.
6. ___Chagrin___ is a feeling of disappointment, upset, or annoyance, perhaps because of your own failure.
7. A ___congenial___ person, place, or environment is pleasant.
8. If something ___invalidates___ something such as a law, contract, or election, it causes it to be considered illegal.
9. The more they ___probe___ into his background, the more inflamed their suspicions would become.
10. ___Conceit___ is associated with stupidity and ignorance.
11. He avoids any eye contact, quickly ___averts___ his gaze when anyone approaches.
12. Talent, hard work and sheer ___tenacity___ are all crucial to career success.
13. A well ___devoid___ of water is useless.
14. ___Abduction___ is the criminal act of capturing and carrying away by force a family member.
15. A person or institution that has ___clout___ has influence and power.
16. ___Covert___ activities or situations are secret or hidden.
17. Keeping the garden tidy all year round can be a ___laborious___ task.
18. ___Indignation___ is a feeling of shock and anger when you think that something is unjust or unfair.
19. ___Ignominy___ is shame or public disgrace.
20. If you ___scrutinize___ something, you examine it very carefully, often to find out some information from it or about it.

Exercise 19-C 偏难词自测练习 (30 minutes)

Please fill in the blanks, choosing the words from the list. Each word can only be used once. Then you can go back to the Word List and check your answers.

请从表格所列单词中选出与下列中文意思对应的单词，填入空格，每个单词只能使用一次。完毕之后，请回到《SAT巴朗词表：乱序版》中对应的单元，核对答案，并标注自己没有填对的单词。

Word List

subjective	encompass	exacting	axiom	concentric
subtlety	duration	allege	furor	sarcasm
mishap	compile	mentor	cohesion	rectitude
irreconcilable	resolve	advocate	impartial	propagate
converse	sham	disclose	bohemian	concoct
insubstantial	articulate	swerve	porous	impassable
immaculate	coup	pithy	induce	flux
unerringly	witless	headstrong	raze	goad
obligatory	whet	impair	effectual	heyday
biased	equinox	gravity	chimerical	provisional
enunciate	clench	conclusive	proxy	
regime	corporeal	enhance	capacity	
facile	quixotic	concur	extenuate	

决心，决定 resolve

有孔的，能渗透的 porous

同中心的 concentric

严格要求的 exacting

不幸的事；灾难 mishap

全盛期，年富力强时期 heyday

容易的；现成的；肤浅的 facile

善于表达的，表达清晰的 articulate

无过失地，正确地 unerringly

突然而巧妙的行动，成功的一举 coup

身体的；物质的 corporeal

相反的事物；谈话 converse

突然转向 swerve

紧握 clench

正直，公正 rectitude

使受损，削弱 extenuate

昼夜平分点；春分；秋分 equinox

驱策，激励；唆使，煽动 goad

（清晰地）发音 enunciate

决定性的；确凿的 conclusive

顽固的，任性的 headstrong

宣称，断言 allege

调制；捏造 concoct

汇编，编辑 compile

同意，一致 concur

挖苦，讽刺 sarcasm

不实在的，非实质的；脆弱的 insubstantial

提倡，拥护 advocate

公理，原则 axiom

劝诱，促使，导致 induce

环绕，包围 encompass

有约束力的；必须的 obligatory

结合，结合力，团结 cohesion

无知的，愚蠢的 witless

夷平，拆毁 raze

微妙；精明；巧妙 subtlety

放荡不羁的 bohemian

不能通行的；不可逾越的 impassable

临时的 provisional

减轻，减少 extenuate

涨潮；变迁 flux

政体，政权 regime

增强，提高；改进 enhance

洁净的；没有缺点的；完美无瑕的 immaculate

繁殖；宣传 propagate

佯装 sham

导师，指导者 mentor

持续期间 duration

堂吉诃德式的，狂想的 auixotic

不能和解的，不相容的 irreconcilable

使…显露，揭露 disclose

激怒，狂热 furor

磨快；刺激，使兴奋 whet

严重性 gravity

有偏见的 biased

公平的，不偏不倚的 impartial

有效的，奏效的 effectual

精炼的，简洁的，精辟的 pithy

异想天开的，空想的 chimerical

主观的，个人的 subjective

代理人 proxy

能力；角色；容量 capacity

Review: Word List 20

- □ belated
- □ accolade
- □ peerless
- □ dissuade
- □ soliloquy
- □ pedagogy
- □ visionary
- □ amphibian
- □ forte
- □ indisputable
- □ bleak
- □ default
- □ estranged
- □ insinuate
- □ recuperate
- □ frail
- □ penitent
- □ spurious
- □ philanthropist
- □ assert
- □ perpetrate
- □ dubious
- □ inkling
- □ foreshadow
- □ presumptuous
- □ episodic
- □ contend
- □ trespass
- □ fruition
- □ inefficacious
- □ underscore
- □ augment
- □ embryonic
- □ quadruped
- □ avocation
- □ devout
- □ chronicle
- □ abysmal
- □ cynical
- □ aromatic
- □ subordinate
- □ embark
- □ synthesis
- □ cohere
- □ diffidence
- □ erratic
- □ vogue
- □ spontaneity
- □ gaudy
- □ composure
- □ intervene
- □ impervious
- □ nadir
- □ headlong
- □ disengage
- □ extent
- □ improvident
- □ empathy
- □ linguistic
- □ contaminate
- □ therapeutic
- □ skimp
- □ enigma
- □ bequeath
- □ transient
- □ steadfast
- □ defer
- □ hierarchy
- □ allay
- □ belittle
- □ eminent
- □ expository
- □ commensurate
- □ outspoken
- □ abolish
- □ sobriety
- □ equity
- □ corollary
- □ introvert
- □ sanctuary
- □ confirm
- □ extricate
- □ slovenly
- □ daunt
- □ felicitous
- □ capacious
- □ fluster
- □ substantial
- □ ignoble
- □ ecstasy
- □ peremptory
- □ impromptu
- □ simile
- □ oracular
- □ fluency
- □ infraction
- □ anchor
- □ chisel
- □ certitude
- □ unassailable

Exercise 20

Exercise 20-A Multiple-Choice Quiz (5 minutes)

Please choose the best answer that conveys the meaning of the given word. There is only one correct choice.
请根据所给单词的意思，从A,B,C,D四个选项中找出其同义词，每题只有一个正确答案。

1. devout (*adj*)
A. inefficacious
B. belated
C. frail
D. pious

2. perpetrate (*v*)
A. render
B. commit
C. assert
D. contend

3. composure (*n*)
A. resignation
B. extent
C. compound
D. calmness

4. trespass (*v*)
A. distinguish
B. underscore
C. invade
D. contaminate

5. erratic (*adj*)
A. odd
B. false
C. therapeutic
D. linguistic

6. augment (*v*)
A. embark
B. cohere
C. intervene
D. increase

7. headlong (*adj*)
A. headstrong
B. desolate
C. hasty
D. eminent

8. commensurate (*adj*)
A. outspoken
B. equal
C. capacious
D. substantial

9. cynical (*adj*)
A. plaintive
B. skeptical
C. imperious
D. embryonic

10. subordinate (*adj*)
A. indisputable
B. inferior
C. dubious
D. episodic

11. penitent (*adj*)
A. defensive
B. bacterial
C. repentant
D. predatory

12. bleak (*adj*)
A. cold
B. empirical
C. incongruous
D. influential

13. default (*n*)
A. failure
B. amphibian
C. diffidence
D. fruition

14. enigma (*n*)
A. spontaneity
B. simile
C. mystery
D. fluency

15. aromatic (*adj*)
A. manipulative
B. fragrant
C. even
D. stunted

16. spurious (*adj*)
A. military
B. thriving
C. counterfeit
D. fulfilled

17. presumptuous (*adj*)
A. expansive
B. suspicious
C. jaded
D. peremptory

18. accolade (*n*)
A. empathy
B. anchor
C. award
D. recruit

19. visionary (*adj*)
A. hereditary
B. fanciful
C. clement
D. mature

20. peerless (*adj*)
A. incomparable
B. incongruous
C. insignificant
D. incorrect

Exercise 20-B Matching Quiz (5 minutes)

Match the words from the two columns.
从右边列表中选出和左边单词意思匹配的词汇，把它们用线连起来。

A

estranged	thriftless
foreshadow	separate
diffidence	alienated
impervious	shyness
nadir	bottom
disengage	impenetrable
improvident	portend

B

extricate	leave
bequeath	temporary
transient	explanatory
allay	cancel
expository	pacify
abolish	free

C

fluster	unprepared
infraction	rapture
impromptu	violation
certitude	confuse
ecstasy	certainty

Exercise 19-C 偏难词自测练习 (30 minutes)

Please fill in the blanks, choosing the words from the list. Each word can only be used once. Then you can go back to the Word List and check your answers.
请从表格所列单词中选出与下列中文意思对应的单词，填入空格，每个单词只能使用一次。完毕之后，请回到《SAT巴朗词表：乱序版》中对应的单元，核对答案，并标注自己没有填对的单词。

Word List

belated	inkling	cohere	hierarchy	capacious
dissuade	episodic	vogue	belittle	substantial
soliloquy	contend	spontaneity	eminent	ignoble
pedagogy	fruition	gaudy	outspoken	peremptory
amphibian	inefficacious	intervene	sobriety	simile
forte	underscore	extent	equity	oracular
indisputable	embryonic	empathy	corollary	fluency
insinuate	quadruped	linguistic	introvert	anchor
recuperate	avocation	contaminate	sanctuary	chisel
frail	chronicle	therapeutic	confirm	unassailable
philanthropist	abysmal	skimp	slovenly	
assert	embark	steadfast	daunt	
dubious	synthesis	defer	felicitous	

深不可测的，无底的 abysmal

流利，流畅 fluency

等级制度；等级森严的组织 hierarchy

两栖类动物 amphibian

开始，着手做；使上船、飞机 embark

大量的；坚固的；实质的 substantial

副业 avocation

同情，同感 empathy

虚弱的 frail

性格内向的人 introvert

黏合 cohere

引起怀疑的；疑惑的，未决的 dubious

结果 corollary

明白的，无争论余地的 indisputable

宽敞的 capacious

坦率的，直言不讳的 outspoken

暗示，旁敲侧击地说；迂回 insinuate

恰当的，贴切的 felicitous

把…系住或扎牢，使固定 anchor

少给，克扣；节约使用 skimp

威吓 daunt

避难所，庇护所；圣堂 sanctuary

自发性；（举止等的）自然 spontaneity

程度；广度；范围 extent

记录，记载（按时间顺序）chronicle

证实，确认，加强 confirm

自言自语，独白 soliloquy

专横的，不容分说的 peremptory

斗争；竞争；声称 contend

艳丽的，俗丽的 gaudy

四足动物 quadruped

结果实；成就；实现 fruition

复原，恢复 recuperate

萌芽阶段的，初步的 embryonic

不修边幅的，懒散的 slovenly

不灵的，无效的 inefficacious

污染 contaminate

明喻 simile

劝…不做某事 dissuade

清醒；严肃；冷静 sobriety

凿子；欺骗，用凿子凿 chisel

强调，加强 underscore

教学；教育学 pedagogy

轻视；贬低 belittle

由许多松散片段组成的 episodic

卑鄙的，卑贱的 ignoble

干涉，介入 intervene

时尚，流行物 vogue

综合，合成 synthesis

断言，坚持己见 assert

（对正在或即将发生的事）略知 inkling

推迟，拖延；缓召，缓役；遵从，服从 defer

特长，专长 forte

著名的，出众的 eminent

语言的，语言学的 linguistic

慈善家，乐善好施者 philanthropist

忠实的；坚贞不移的 steadfast

迟到的 belated

公平，公正 equity

治疗的，治疗学的 therapeutic

无可争辩的；攻不破的 unassailable

神圣预言的；神谕似的；神谕的 oracular

Review: Word Lists 21&22

- □ energize
- □ archetype
- □ attain
- □ novelty
- □ weather
- □ quibble
- □ impropriety
- □ irony
- □ muted
- □ libel
- □ excise
- □ overwrought
- □ nemesis
- □ retribution
- □ carping
- □ arousal
- □ parochial
- □ polemical
- □ affluence
- □ aristocracy
- □ evenhanded
- □ degenerate
- □ deflect
- □ censure
- □ absorb
- □ imbalance
- □ irksome
- □ cajole
- □ exorbitant
- □ relegate
- □ biennial
- □ epic
- □ prey
- □ frivolous
- □ boycott
- □ ominous
- □ practical
- □ monarchy
- □ dogmatic
- □ implication
- □ blithe
- □ torpor
- □ farce
- □ parable
- □ cursory
- □ incoherence
- □ devise
- □ sadistic
- □ incumbent
- □ illusory
- □ embroil
- □ catholic
- □ chronic
- □ salvage
- □ trite
- □ sustenance
- □ marred
- □ atlas
- □ momentous
- □ obscure
- □ seemly
- □ averse
- □ abusive
- □ abridge
- □ cache
- □ indulgent
- □ taciturn
- □ commiserate
- □ withstand
- □ confiscate
- □ vie
- □ prevalent
- □ meager
- □ officious
- □ contempt
- □ eclectic
- □ kudos
- □ monolithic
- □ indiscretion
- □ patronize
- □ befuddle
- □ repugnant
- □ profane
- □ exploit
- □ transgression
- □ jeopardize
- □ purge
- □ nuance
- □ disdain
- □ precept
- □ contemporary
- □ brittle
- □ sinewy
- □ heedless
- □ figurative
- □ precise
- □ glib
- □ conifer
- □ insulated
- □ franchise
- □ improvise
- □ foment
- □ irrefutable
- □ skiff
- □ ironic
- □ address
- □ discredit
- □ debunk
- □ demagogue
- □ decorum
- □ jargon
- □ tirade
- □ dint
- □ surmise
- □ anonymity
- □ introspective
- □ treatise
- □ prodigious
- □ retort
- □ disquiet
- □ dumbfound
- □ deluge
- □ pact
- □ stock
- □ concrete
- □ generalization
- □ afford
- □ synthetic
- □ charismatic
- □ speculate
- □ likelihood
- □ commandeer
- □ concentration
- □ definition
- □ detachment
- □ discernible
- □ elaboration
- □ thesis
- □ facility
- □ hinder
- □ adopt
- □ medium
- □ reflect
- □ solution

Exercises 21&22

Exercise 21-A Multiple-Choice Quiz (5 minutes)

Please choose the best answer that conveys the meaning of the given word. There is only one correct choice.
请根据所给单词的意思，从A,B,C,D四个选项中找出其同义词，每题只有一个正确答案。

1. carping (*adj*)
   A. expostulatory
   B. practical
   C. critical
   D. sadistic

2. embroil (*v*)
   A. involve
   B. vanish
   C. devise
   D. obscure

3. boycott (*v*)
   A. reign
   B. coax
   C. regiment
   D. reject

4. blithe (*adj*)
   A. appropriate
   B. joyous
   C. communicative
   D. loose

5. cajole (*v*)
   A. interact
   B. enact
   C. coax
   D. validate

6. frivolous (*adj*)
   A. continuous
   B. unimportant
   C. rolling
   D. spectacular

7. irksome (*adj*)
   A. annoying
   B. inherited
   C. vehement
   D. restless

8. ominous (*adj*)
   A. furious
   B. subtle
   C. sinister
   D. sedentary

9. censure (*v*)
   A. trail
   B. rebuke
   C. pollinate
   D. emulate

10. muted (*adj*)
    A. bluff
    B. magnetic
    C. ironic
    D. silent

11. cursory (*adj*)
A. superficial
B. irrefutable
C. abusive
D. prevalent

12. farce (*n*)
A. likelihood
B. definition
C. mockery
D. detachment

13. marred (*adj*)
A. seductive
B. damaged
C. concrete
D. synthetic

14. trite (*adj*)
A. cliché
B. sublime
C. ponderous
D. inauspicious

15. relegate (*v*)
A. abridge
B. permit
C. degrade
D. swing

16. deflect (*v*)
A. discompose
B. reflect
C. repute
D. deviate

17. polemical (*adj*)
A. tidal
B. critical
C. intent
D. tonal

18. libel (*n*)
A. deliberation
B. arousal
C. affluence
D. slander

19. weather (*v*)
A. endure
B. improvise
C. disquiet
D. compromise

20. archetype (*n*)
A. solution
B. facility
C. original
D. concentration

Exercises 21&22-B Matching Quiz (5 minutes)

Match the words from the two columns.
从右边列表中选出和左边单词意思匹配的词汇，把它们用线连起来。

A

excise	revenge
overwrought	impartial
retribution	broad
parochial	opinionated
evenhanded	nervous
dogmatic	delete
parable	provincial
incumbent	allegory
catholic	obligatory

B

salvage	maps
sustenance	proper
atlas	nourishment
momentous	antipathetic
seemly	hideout
averse	sympathize
cache	lenient
indulgent	rescue
commiserate	consequential
withstand	champion
patronize	desecrate
profane	feat
exploit	resist

C

jeopardize	distinction
purge	right
nuance	superficial
disdain	purify
precept	rule
brittle	fragile
glib	contempt
franchise	endanger

D

address	tackle
discredit	terminology
debunk	speculate
decorum	medium
jargon	expose
dint	defame
surmise	dissertation
treatise	propriety

E

retort	commonplace
pact	appealing
stock	treaty
charismatic	reply
discernible	perceivable
hinder	enormous
prodigious	hamper

Exercises 21&22-C 偏难词自测练习 (30 minutes)

Please fill in the blanks, choosing the words from the list. Each word can only be used once. Then you can go back to the Word List and check your answers.
请从表格所列单词中选出与下列中文意思对应的单词，填入空格，每个单词只能使用一次。完毕之后，请回到《SAT巴朗词表：乱序版》中对应的单元，核对答案，并标注自己没有填对的单词。

Word List

energize	prey	prevalent	conifer	afford
attain	practical	meager	insulated	synthetic
novelty	monarchy	officious	improvise	speculate
quibble	implication	contempt	foment	likelihood
impropriety	torpor	eclectic	irrefutable	commandeer
irony	incoherence	kudos	skiff	concentration
nemesis	devise	monolithic	ironic	definition
arousal	sadistic	indiscretion	demagogue	detachment
affluence	illusory	befuddle	tirade	elaboration
aristocracy	chronic	repugnant	anonymity	thesis
degenerate	obscure	transgression	introspective	facility
absorb	abusive	contemporary	disquiet	adopt
imbalance	abridge	sinewy	dumbfound	medium
exorbitant	taciturn	heedless	deluge	reflect
biennial	confiscate	figurative	concrete	solution
epic	vie	precise	generalization	

君主政体；君主制国家 monarchy

不适当，不合适 impropriety

深思熟虑；表达；反射 reflect

衰退，堕落，变坏 degenerate

以达到私欲为目的的煽动者，蛊惑性政客 demagogue

被掠食者，猎物；牺牲者 prey

合成的；人造的 synthetic

竞争，较量 vie

辱骂的；虐待的 abusive

使不安，使忧虑 disquiet

普遍的，流行的 prevalent

新奇；新奇的事物 novelty

同时代的人；当代的；同时代的，属于同一时期的 contemporary

慢性的 chronic

激起；鼓励 foment

富裕，富足 affluence

征用；强占 commandeer

两年一次的 biennial

幻觉的，迷惑人的 illusory

使惊讶，使吃惊 dumbfound

不注意的 heedless

能力；灵巧；设备 facility

使精力充沛，使充满活力 energize

比喻的，修辞丰富的 figurative

残酷成性的 sadistic

吹毛求疵的异议 quibble

概论；一般化 generalization

没收，征用 confiscate

讽刺的，啼笑皆非的 ironic

实践的，实用的 practical

匿名 anonymity

暗示的东西 implication

使迷惑 befuddle

解决；溶液 solution

长篇的激烈演说；长篇的攻击性演说 tirade

方法；培养液；手法，手段 medium

不活泼；迟钝；冬眠 torpor

可能性 likelihood

违法，犯罪 transgression

贵族；贵族阶级 aristocracy

与世隔绝的 insulated

过分的，过高的 exorbitant

定义；清晰度；轮廓 definition

好管闲事的 officious

不连贯；没有条理 incoherence

超然；派遣；分开 detachment

暗讽；反语 irony

小船，单人小艇 skiff

精确的，准确的 precise

集中；聚集；浓度 concentration

有形的；实际的；具体的 concrete

详尽（阐述） elaboration

论文；论点 thesis

同化；吸收；使全神贯注 absorb

不慎重，不明智 indiscretion

沉默寡言的 taciturn

买得起，负担得起；提供 afford

删节，削减，精简 abridge

整体式的；不屈的 monolithic

内省的，反省的 introspective

不平衡 imbalance

推测；投机 speculate

令人讨厌的 repugnant

觉醒；激励 arousal

黑暗的，朦胧的，模糊的；使黑暗，使模糊 obscure

即兴创作 improvise

贫乏的；不足的 meager

坚韧的，强壮有力的 sinewy

达到；获得 attain

奖赏；荣誉；称赞 kudos

无可辩驳的 irrefutable

松类 conifer

兼收并蓄的，博采众长的 eclestic

想出；发明；设计 devise

史诗；叙事诗 epic

洪水，急流；（某事物）泛滥；使泛滥，淹没 deluge

复仇者；强硬对手或敌手 nemesis

收养；采用，采取，采纳；正式接受；批准 adopt

轻视，蔑视 contempt

Answers
答案

Answers

Exercise 1

1-A

1. C
2. A
3. B
4. D
5. B
6. C
7. D
8. A
9. C
10. B
11. A
12. D
13. B
14. A
15. D
16. B
17. C

1-B

1. elusive
2. nonchalance
3. wily
4. alleviate
5. stint
6. opportune
7. emulate
8. indelible
9. contests
10. injurious
11. antiquated
12. meticulous
13. discomposure
14. invulnerable
15. tangential
16. surveillance
17. insubordination
18. fraternize
19. ulterior
20. halting
21. superficial

Exercise 2

2-A

1. B
2. A
3. B
4. A
5. C
6. D
7. D
8. A
9. B
10. C
11. B
12. B
13. C
14. C
15. D
16. A
17. B
18. C
19. D

2-B

1. embellish—ornament
2. analogy—similarity
3. ferment—turmoil
4. compliance—conformity
5. connotation—meaning
6. incorporate—unite
7. ebullient—joyful
8. reciprocal—mutual
9. aversion—dislike
10. conspiracy—plot
11. preeminent—outstanding
12. abate—decrease
13. sovereign—self-governing
14. increment—increase
15. prelude—introduction
16. repel—disgust
17. assent—accept
18. anomaly—irregularity
19. depravity—corruption
20. lucid—intelligible
21. extrapolation—projection
22. premise—postulate
23. render—deliver

Exercise 3

3-A

1. C	4. A	7. B	10. C	13. B	16. C
2. A	5. B	8. C	11. D	14. C	
3. D	6. D	9. C	12. D	15. A	

3-B

1. notoriety	7. stratagem	13. thwarted	19. adulterated
2. discount	8. retracted	14. expedient	20. astute
3. congruent	9. incriminated	15. forum	21. awe
4. liability	10. reputed	16. dictum	
5. cater to	11. apprehension	17. felicity	
6. brandishing	12. domineer	18. ancestry	

Exercise 4

4-A

1. B	4. D	7. A	10. A	13. B	16. A	19. A
2. A	5. B	8. C	11. D	14. C	17. B	20. D
3. A	6. C	9. B	12. A	15. D	18. C	

4-B

1. query—question	6. redundant—superfluous	11. detraction—slander
2. burnish—polish	7. countermand—cancel	12. amenable—deferential
3. admonition—warning	8. parameter—boundary	13. candor—honesty
4. pathetic—pitiful	9. ambience—atmosphere	14. geniality—friendliness
5. comprise—include	10. mitigate—appease	

Exercise 5

5-A

1. D	4. A	7. A	10. C	13. D	16. D	19. B
2. B	5. D	8. C	11. A	14. B	17. D	20. C
3. A	6. D	9. C	12. B	15. B	18. C	21. D

5-B

1. impenetrable
2. realm
3. anonymous
4. denotation
5. recourse
6. surmount
7. unwarranted
8. relinquish
9. cardinal
10. sublime
11. incredulous
12. outmoded
13. ambiguous
14. aloof
15. blundered
16. kindled
17. premeditated
18. malleable
19. prowess
20. relented
21. mediated
22. circumlocution

Exercise 6

6-A

1. C
2. D
3. A
4. B
5. A
6. C
7. A
8. D
9. B
10. C
11. A
12. A
13. C
14. A
15. C
16. B
17. D
18. C
19. B
20. A

6-B

1. ethos—character
2. lexicon—dictionary
3. coercion—compulsion
4. surrogate—substitute
5. unanimity—consensus
6. dispatch—send
7. complacency— self-satisfaction
8. anomalous—irregular
9. prodigy—genius
10. formidable—difficult
11. transport—ecstasy
12. engaging—charming
13. submissive—yielding
14. perverse—irrational
15. withdrawn—introverted
16. dearth—scarcity
17. inexorable—relentless
18. trifling—trivial
19. jovial—merry

Exercise 7

7-A

1. A
2. B
3. C
4. D
5. B
6. C
7. A
8. B
9. A
10. C
11. C
12. C
13. A
14. D
15. B
16. C
17. D
18. B
19. A
20. D
21. C

7-B

1. partitioning
2. atrophy
3. attest
4. congenital
5. predispose
6. Adversity
7. beamed
8. perused
9. derivative
10. fraudulent
11. posthumous
12. quailed

13. adorns
14. loquacious
15. engenders
16. criterion
17. archaic
18. irrevocable
19. foreboding
20. anthology
21. decrepit
22. consolidation

Exercise 8

8-A

1. B
2. D
3. C
4. C
5. A
6. D
7. B
8. D
9. A
10. D
11. B
12. D
13. C
14. D
15. A
16. A
17. B
18. C
19. A
20. C
21. D
22. B

8-B

1. dire—disastrous
2. propitious—favorable
3. remnant—remainder
4. temporize—delay
5. flair—talent
6. theoretical—hypothetical
7. stringent—rigid
8. zeal—enthusiasm
9. equitable—impartial
10. stipulate—specify
11. demur—object
12. industrious—assiduous
13. arable—cultivatable
14. categorical—absolute
15. insurgent—rebellious
16. resentment—indignation
17. manifest—evident
18. conciliatory—reconciling
19. invigorate—energize
20. bizarre—peculiar
21. proliferation—growth
22. constraint—compulsion

Exercise 9

9-A

1. C
2. A
3. D
4. D
5. D
6. A
7. A
8. B
9. B
10. C
11. C
12. A
13. B
14. D
15. A
16. D
17. D
18. B
19. C

9-B

1. cosmopolitan
2. Pathos
3. exigency
4. parody
5. amiable
6. evocative
7. flippant
8. ostensible
9. mendacious
10. Acumen
11. partiality
12. provident
13. plagiarized
14. recession
15. maxim
16. aptitude
17. imminent
18. renovating
19. disparate
20. Lax
21. justification
22. aftermath

Exercise 10

10-A

1. D	4. A	7. A	10. B	13. C	16. D	19. D
2. C	5. B	8. C	11. A	14. B	17. A	20. C
3. A	6. C	9. D	12. D	15. A	18. C	

10-B

1. relic—remains
2. relish—enjoy
3. expansive—sociable
4. obsessive—addictive
5. bountiful—abundant
6. compromise—endanger
7. sagacious—shrewd
8. quaint—eccentric
9. disinterested—impartial
10. voluminous—capacious
11. convoluted—intricate
12. pliant—deferential
13. quizzical—teasing
14. malignant—injurious
15. culminate—climax
16. sedition—insubordination
17. colossal—immense
18. affliction—distress
19. menial—lowly
20. withhold—conceal
21. cataclysm—upheaval
22. impunity—pardon

Exercise 11

11-A

1. C	4. B	7. C	10. D	13. C	16. D	19. A
2. D	5. A	8. D	11. C	14. B	17. C	20. C
3. A	6. C	9. B	12. A	15. D	18. A	21. D

11-B

1. gloss over
2. vantage
3. remonstrance
4. ascertained
5. decipher
6. interminable
7. unwieldy
8. complements
9. resurged
10. negligible
11. insurmountable
12. overbearing
13. resilient
14. disarray
15. platitude
16. unravel
17. uproarious
18. intuition
19. onset
20. nebulous
21. vindictive
22. Opulence
23. unwitting

Exercise 12

12-A

1. A	4. A	7. D	10. A	13. B	16. D	19. C
2. C	5. B	8. C	11. D	14. B	17. C	20. B
3. D	6. C	9. B	12. C	15. A	18. C	21. D

12-B

1. assimilate—absorb
2. intimate—allude
3. diverge—differ
4. appraise—gauge
5. flaunt—show off
6. germinate—sprout
7. baffle—disconcert
8. vex—irritate
9. simulate—feign
10. comprehensive—inclusive
11. cessation—end
12. mimicry—imitation
13. sophisticated—worldly-wise
14. discourse—speech
15. contrived—artificial
16. deadlock—stalemate
17. omnipresent—ubiquitous
18. clamor—noise
19. jubilation—joy
20. undermine—compromise
21. reprisal—retaliation

Exercise 13

13-A

1. B	4. B	7. D	10. C	13. B	16. A	19. B
2. C	5. D	8. A	11. B	14. C	17. A	20. A
3. A	6. C	9. A	12. D	15. D	18. C	

13-B

1. infinitesimal
2. allegiance
3. allocated
4. pensive
5. tribute
6. atrocity
7. propitiate
8. reciprocate
9. volition
10. dutiful
11. wary
12. solemnity
13. wrath
14. tenuous
15. Satire
16. inopportune
17. discriminating
18. savored
19. duped
20. Dissident
21. amicable
22. abdicates
23. unmitigated

Exercise 14

14-A

1. D	4. B	7. D	10. B	13. D	16. C	19. D
2. C	5. A	8. C	11. A	14. A	17. A	
3. A	6. D	9. D	12. A	15. B	18. B	

14-B

1. coagulate—clot
2. monotony—tedium
3. erroneous—incorrect
4. thrifty—economical
5. vigilance—watchfulness
6. altruistic—selfless
7. diffuse—wordy
8. omnipotent—all-powerful
9. flounder—struggle
10. inception—beginning
11. omniscient—all-knowing
12. cession—ceding
13. rapacious—greedy
14. tenacious—persistent
15. collusion—complicity
16. fickle—changeable
17. adept—expert
18. patent—evident
19. acquiesce—assent
20. revulsion—change
21. renounce—abandon
22. coin—fabricate

Exercise 15

15-A

1. C	4. D	7. A	10. B	13. C	16. B	19. B
2. C	5. B	8. D	11. D	14. C	17. D	20. C
3. A	6. C	9. C	12. A	15. D	18. A	

15-B

1. alimentary
2. impasse
3. paramount
4. decimating
5. obviate
6. alienate
7. sanguine
8. illicit
9. nominal
10. sluggish
11. concerted
12. noncommittal
13. Contagion
14. abject
15. vehement
16. inept
17. hoax
18. casualty
19. Tentative
20. countenance
21. proclivity
22. taints
23. demeanor
24. depreciates
25. dispersed

Exercise 16

16-A

1. D	4. A	7. D	10. D	13. A	16. B	19. C
2. A	5. C	8. B	11. C	14. A	17. A	
3. D	6. A	9. C	12. C	15. D	18. A	

16-B

1. amorous—loving
2. hypercritical—overcritical
3. genesis—origin
4. didactic—teaching
5. parasite—freeloader
6. optimum—best
7. flag—droop
8. inarticulate—speechless
9. indubitable—unquestionable
10. imprudent—injudicious
11. heed—consider
12. inveterate—deep-rooted
13. disgruntle—dissatisfy
14. prophetic—foreshadowing
15. exceptionable—objectionable
16. perturb—disturb
17. misconstrue—misjudge
18. disenfranchise—deprive
19. defiance—resistance
20. amity—friendship
21. levy—impose
22. buoyant—cheerful
23. linger—dawdle

Exercise 17

17-A

1. D	4. B	7. D	10. A	13. C	16. A	19. A
2. B	5. A	8. B	11. B	14. D	17. A	
3. C	6. C	9. A	12. C	15. C	18. B	

17-B

1. provocative
2. impediment
3. docile
4. emancipated
5. mushrooms
6. atone
7. has subsided
8. edict
9. woe
10. desolate
11. marshaled
12. juncture
13. stigma
14. Judicious
15. ruminate
16. sinister
17. has faltered
18. tacit
19. ratify
20. banal
21. callous
22. supersede
23. boisterous
24. repressed

Exercise 18

18-A

1. C
2. A
3. D
4. B
5. D
6. C
7. B
8. D
9. C
10. C
11. A
12. A
13. B
14. D
15. D
16. C
17. C

18-B

1. delve—dig
2. monumental—massive
3. antecede—precede
4. dissertation—essay
5. protract—prolong
6. contingent—conditional
7. anecdote—story
8. exult—rejoice
9. prologue—introduction
10. analogous—comparable
11. ruthless—cruel
12. subterfuge—trickery
13. exhaustive—comprehensive
14. catastrophe—calamity
15. knotty—intricate
16. collate—compare
17. commemorate—celebrate
18. sporadic—occasional
19. brusque—abrupt
20. trivial—trifling
21. prognosis—forecast

Exercise 19

19-A

1. A
2. C
3. D
4. B
5. B
6. D
7. A
8. B
9. C
10. D
11. B
12. A
13. A
14. B
15. D
16. D
17. B
18. D
19. A

19-B

1. seasoned
2. Homage
3. disparage
4. inscrutable
5. muster
6. Chagrin
7. congenial
8. invalidates
9. probe
10. Conceit
11. averting
12. tenacity
13. devoid
14. Abduction
15. clout
16. Covert
17. laborious
18. Indignation
19. Ignominy
20. scrutinize

Exercise 20

20-A

1. D
2. B
3. D
4. C
5. A
6. D
7. C
8. B
9. B
10. B
11. C
12. A
13. A
14. C
15. B
16. C
17. D
18. C
19. B
20. A

20-B

1. estranged—alienated
2. foreshadow—portend
3. diffidence—shyness
4. impervious—impenetrable
5. nadir—bottom
6. disengage—separate
7. improvident—thriftless
8. extricate—free
9. bequeath—leave
10. transient—temporary
11. allay—pacify
12. expository—explanatory
13. abolish—cancel
14. fluster—confuse
15. infraction—violation
16. impromptu—unprepared
17. certitude—certainty
18. ecstasy—rapture

Exercises 21&22

21-A

1. C
2. A
3. D
4. B
5. C
6. B
7. A
8. C
9. B
10. D
11. A
12. C
13. B
14. A
15. C
16. D
17. B
18. D
19. A
20. C

21&22-B

1. excise—delete
2. overwrought—nervous
3. retribution—revenge
4. parochial—provincial
5. evenhanded—impartial
6. dogmatic—opinionated
7. parable—allegory
8. incumbent—obligatory
9. catholic—broad
10. salvage—rescue
11. sustenance—nourishment
12. atlas—maps
13. momentous—consequential
14. seemly—proper
15. averse—antipathetic
16. cache—hideout
17. indulgent—lenient
18. commiserate—sympathize
19. withstand—resist
20. patronize—champion
21. profane—desecrate
22. exploit—feat
23. jeopardize—endanger
24. purge—purify
25. nuance—distinction
26. disdain—contempt
27. precept—rule
28. brittle—fragile
29. glib—fluent
30. franchise—right
31. address—tackle
32. discredit—defame
33. debunk—expose
34. decorum—propriety
35. jargon—terminology
36. dint—medium
37. surmise—speculate
38. treatise—dissertation
39. retort—reply
40. pact—treaty
41. stock—commonplace
42. charismatic—appealing
43. discernible—perceivable
44. hinder—hamper
45. prodigious—enormous